OUT OF
THIRTY-FIVE YEARS

From the painting by Albert Herter.

Samuel Tuxler

OUT OF
THIRTY-FIVE YEARS

*Being leaves from the Life Book of a
Lutheran pastor who looks out
on the World and sees both
Good and Evil.*

BY

SAMUEL TREXLER

AUTHOR OF
Crusaders of the Twentieth Century.

G. P. PUTNAM'S SONS
New York :: London
1936

Printed in the United States of America

To My Gentle Mother

WHOSE LOVE AND STRENGTH ENCOMPASS
ME AS THEY DID THROUGHOUT THESE
THIRTY-FIVE YEARS.

PREFACE

THE Church is facing trying conditions. In the next few years she will be tested more thoroughly than she has been tested since the days of the prophets and the martyrs. The most important link in the religious life is the minister; people will follow where they are rightly led. Because of this fact I have made it of first importance both in official acts and in personal contacts to strengthen the ministry of the Church. It must be more carefully selected, more thoroughly trained. Times without number I have listened to a church board battling with its almost insuperable problems of keeping a church alive only to discover that the congregation had been struggling with a pastor who was ill-fitted for his work. The pastor was probably working up to his ability, but that ability was limited. The one method whereby the Church can meet the problems of the future is to have a superior ministry. To this end have I written this book, and it is my hope that it will be of some value in accomplishing that great purpose.

SAMUEL TREXLER.

January, 1936

CONTENTS

FOUR of these chapters formed a series of lectures delivered to the students of the Lutheran Theological Seminary at Philadelphia in March 1935. The chapter on "The Church and Youth" was a paper read at the Third Lutheran World Convention, Paris, France, October 1935.

OUT OF
THIRTY-FIVE YEARS

CHAPTER ONE

THE MINISTER IN THE MODERN WORLD

My father was a man of giant frame. A wide margin of physical strength allowed him to minister for forty-six years to four scattered churches lying along the Blue Mountains of Pennsylvania. In the heat of summer and the cold of winter he traveled slowly at a time when there were no automobiles. He traveled along the unimproved country roads in the spring thaw; and when the roads were so drifted by the winter's snow that the only safe way to travel was through the open fields. Today as I go along those roads, now improved, I am always reminded of a journey I took with him in his sleigh before I was six years old. To keep one of his Sunday appointments twenty miles away he started one Saturday afternoon to make this five hours' journey. Despite the buffalo robe, a friend to the entire family, we had difficulty in withstanding the cold, which became more and more intense as the sun went down. We finally stopped at a country store, where he bought a box on which I sat between his legs. Tucked in there I kept warm until we reached the home of a hospitable parishioner, where we spent the night in a room that was rarely occupied and never heated.

Such experiences were common, not only on Sundays but on weekdays, on my father's tours of his parish ministry. His moral strength rivaled his physical energy, and it is not surprising that such a man should have left a deep impression upon his three sons—Martin, the oldest; myself; and Charles, the youngest. He had dedicated all three of us to the ministry before we were born, and the whole of our childhood and youth tended in that direction so far as he was able to determine it. Certainly the ministry of the Gospel seemed to be the vocation that drew me, and when I for a short time looked into the law to test myself, I found the greater satisfaction to lie in the call of the ministry. Through my father's influence I felt secure in an apostolic succession which no episcopal hands could enhance.

My father was severe, and his severity consisted in exact discipline. During the summer holidays we were not allowed to invite our souls to idle ease but were compelled to work on a near-by farm, rising with the farmers at half-past four in the morning. His care for our education extended to securing everything, often at great sacrifice to himself and to my mother, that would help promote it. In those days of limited travel he was a happy abettor and accomplice in every trip that I longed for. He sent his three boys in 1893 to see the wonders of the World's Fair in

Chicago, which at that time seemed to symbolize the entrance into a new age. In my college days he provided a purse of $50 which would carry me through New England, including a week at Northfield, where I had my first contact with that remarkable man of God, Dwight L. Moody. Boston, Newport, and New York were new territory to the youth hungry for knowledge and experience.

In this way the call to the ministry came to me. It was like many other experiences of my life—a growing conviction. The statement of St. Paul, "Woe is me if I preach not the Gospel," would not describe my conviction. I had to grow into it. It was a calm, clear call, not contested by many other interests. It was mediated directly through my father, who both by example and by precept was unfailing in his devotion to the Gospel ministry.

The testimonies of my ministerial friends again and again reveal the influence of a father in directing his son's thoughts toward the Christian ministry. "My earliest associations centered around the Church in which my father, grandfather, and several members of the Cadman family were preachers and pastors," stated the Rev. Dr. S. Parkes Cadman, whose writings and radio addresses are known throughout the world. Growing under this influence, the time came, at sixteen years of age, when he publicly confessed Christ as Lord and Redeemer. "That act was the consummation of careful training and of a prolonged period of anxious personal desire to do God's will," Dr. Cadman told me. "Since that decisive experience I have had not the slightest wish to retract or retreat. Quite otherwise, its influence has dominated my entire career, which I would unhesitatingly select again had I to make a choice."

And again. "Originally I suppose my call grew out of the deep devotion I had, and still have, to my father, who is a successful pastor in the American Lutheran Church," wrote the Rev. Dr. Armin George Weng, pastor of Holy Trinity Lutheran Church, Elgin, Illinois. "I felt that his life was so eminently worth while that I hoped mine might be worth while too."

The father of the Rev. Russell F. Auman, of Church of the Redeemer, Scarsdale, New York, disappointed in not realizing his own dream of entering the ministry, cherished the hope that his son would become a pastor. His eyes filled with the tears of joy when the son, after long thought and prayer, made the great decision.

One of the great difficulties in the experience of the skeptic is that of accepting the reality of a call to the Christian ministry. The modern world appears to hold no place for the minister. Twentieth-century life is made up of speed and noise and action; it leaves little time for introspection. It offers nothing to the inner life, the existence of which can readily be ignored by vast groups of men. The invitations and promises of the lowly Nazarene appear to have no bearing on the life of our day. In such a world as this, why should anyone wish to be a minister?

Incomprehensible, but real! The call still comes! It comes because the world still needs the minister, the man who serves. Speed is not an end in itself; modern discoveries and inventions, incredibly wonderful as some of them are, are not ends in themselves. In a world of things, and the multiplication of things, there must be men to remind their fellows that these can be both good and evil. An airplane may carry a sick man to a hospital or a bomb for release upon a city to destroy homes and lives. Science with almost inhuman detachment shows how to use gases to save life or to kill. The minister is the man who must give meaning to all these discoveries, stressing their usefulness in the lives of men. Just as modern developments in the physical world have given a new meaning to speed, so also have they given a new meaning to service. Undirected or misdirected inventions may destroy our twentieth-century civilization unless consecrated men, devoted to the service of their fellows, show how they can be used in a civilized way—how they can be used in the arts of peace and not of war.

His call to the ministry and the life of my friend, the Rev. Dr. Harry Emerson Fosdick, pastor of the Riverside Church, New York, will illustrate what I mean. "I came from a Christian home where the ideal of service was steadfastly taught and exhibited," he told me. "It never would have occurred to us that a worthy life could have any other aim than human service. In my youth I had a thoroughgoing evangelical Christian experience—an experience of great need, great salvation, great gratitude, and great devotion. Out of this came the desire to devote my life to some specific spiritual contribution to my generation." In the fulfillment of that desire he found himself called to the ministry, and in his work at the Riverside Church he is making that spiritual contribution which the world needs.

The real test of a call as a human experience is the personal test. "God's call to me was not a single cry but a still small voice always present in my soul," the Rev. Dr. F. H. Knubel, President of the United Lutheran Church, told me. From childhood up he had experiences that pointed the way to his final conviction that "nothing else seemed worth while doing in life aside from the proclamation of the Saviour."

From time to time I have met a young Presbyterian minister, the Rev. Edwin Kennedy, formerly of West Orange, now of Christ Presbyterian Church, Madison, Wisconsin, whose whole personality is a perpetual witness to the reality of his call. It started with his love as a child for the Church; it developed through the influence of a minister, who, however, uttered the warning in a sermon that no one should become a preacher unless "he would rather preach than eat." At college he was reasonably certain of the call, which finally came in front of the small white church of a village through which he was passing.

"I visualized myself in that or some similar place, living in relation to the people in much the same way as the village doctor. One would be their guide, philosopher, and friend. There would be serenity in one's surroundings, a sense of usefulness in oneself, and an aura of friendliness over all. For the rest of that day there was a quiet ecstasy which permeated my whole being, and a joyous sense of knowing definitely the course that lay before me."

Sometimes men try to avoid the call—only to surrender finally. From the point of view of our search for evidence as to the reality of a call, this experience may be regarded as of even greater value than the call which found the man ready to respond. Actually this is not so, but the call that encounters obstacles has this advantage—it does not represent a hasty inclination. Such a call must have sufficient power to turn a man from another course toward which he is inclined.

I am thinking of the experience of a well-known New York clergyman, a distinguished preacher, whose name must remain anonymous. He told me how he grew up in the home of an English clergyman, where he resented all the petty friction and grievances that came to his father.

"I resolved not to become a minister," he said. "I went through college and university resolved to enter some other vocation. I took the Civil Service examinations and flunked, although I had taken highest honors during my scholastic training. I took a second Civil Service examination, and again flunked—showing that my heart was not in it. After several years of this trying to find myself I finally yielded to the inward urge and decided to enter the ministry. I immediately felt a liberation of myself. During my contact with my father I had dwelt too much on the smaller, annoying side, and possibly was not acquainted enough with the positive value of the vocation."

In the times of the prophets the call often came directly through vision or voice to men to speak for God. In these later days, in the era of the Church, this call comes mostly through the servants of the Church. Woe to him through whom a young man is turned away from the ministry! Upon us pastors rests the very serious responsibility of not urging men into the ministry who are unfitted for this calling; on the other hand, it is tragic if through our flippancy or cynicism worthy men are turned away from their goal. Upon us so largely depends the continuation of the ministry for future generations. Throughout a long period of yearly examinations of men who are entering the ministry I have found a large number drawn thither by the influence of some pastor. Happy the pastor who, perhaps unconsciously, has been the instrument for releasing in some gifted young man abounding powers for Christ and His Church.

Assuming that a call to the ministry is a reality in human experience, the question still arises: How can any particular call be tested? Even while the Church maintains that men throughout the ages have heard and answered the call, it does not follow that she must believe immediately every man who comes along and says he has a call. She has a right to test that call, and she exercises the right. The method may vary, but in the Protestant churches the common practice is to invite the candidate for the ministry to appear before an Examining Committee.

I have not sat all these years on examining committees without realizing that this method of testing a young man's call is fallible, but I am quite sure that the work of such committees has value. I am not thinking merely of doctrinal tests but of the facts concerning character and personality that emerge when the candidate is interviewed. In past days his educational qualifications were investigated, but today he is presumed to be sufficiently educated after his courses at college and seminary.

When a young man asks for the support of the Church to see him through his period of education the committee appointed to examine him is much more thorough. The expense of his training is involved. A man has to be in a position to prove that he has a call before he passes that committee successfully!

One must not overlook the power of self-deception. Even the man who thinks himself most consecrated may ultimately find himself mistaken as to his call. Many large business houses test a man at the end of a ten-year term in their employ. Is he fit to continue? Or are his gifts such that he would be more adequately used at some other employment? The latter judgment may seem very harsh at the time, but it guarantees advantage to both employee and employer. I have increasingly felt the value of being honest in such matters. Would not the Church do well to encourage young men who have been in the ministry for five or ten years to examine themselves, with the aid of facilities given them by the Church, to see whether they should continue in their ministry? How many a man would find himself lacking in natural equipment or in grace and would thereby avoid the shipwreck of his own life and of congregation after congregation! A man can honestly serve elsewhere if he finds himself mistaken in his initial pursuit. His fellow men will esteem him more highly if in the pliable period of his life he changes his vocation when he finds he is unfitted for the ministry of the Gospel. On the other hand, a man may experiment with other callings before he finally finds his lifework in the Christian ministry. The

Rev. Dr. Ralph W. Sockman, wishing to enter
some "service" vocation, inclined first toward an
academic rather than an ecclesiastical career—
but he found himself in ministering to the Methodist Episcopal congregation at Christ Church,
Park Avenue, New York. "I feel that the ministry must be a combination of self-analysis and
a sense of divine mission," was the way he described his call to me. "The longer I am in the
work the more I feel that it is the place where I
can best put in my service." The Rev. Dr. Paul
Scherer of Holy Trinity Lutheran Church, New
York, who has a great following among young
people in the Church, entered the seminary after
a quick decision against medicine, for which he
was preparing. "I am conscious now, as I was
not then, of the Hand that was on the wheel of
my ship," he stated.

Men are often unfitted for a successful ministry
by trifling circumstances. The Protestant
Church is still very young in her organization;
she can use a man only if he has a modicum of
ability to preach, to care for souls, and to administer a parish. A man may be richly endowed in
two of these vocations, but if he lacks the third
his ministry is anathema. So we lose men who
are highly gifted along one line only. The
Roman Catholic Church, with her superior organization, is able to enrich her ranks by the in-
clusion of such men. For instance, a man may
contribute to the scholarship of the Church who

is not at all fitted to preach and to mingle sympathetically with his people. Such instances are repeated again and again. Or a man may have a heart of sympathy for his fellows and not have the gift of preaching; if our ministry of mercy were developed this man would be able to use his talents to the utmost. Likewise a man of teaching ability would be useful in the parish even though he cannot attract great congregations. The fault lies in our failure to develop our parishes in their great ministry. Such developments would mean the parish's rising to its great possibilities. It would mean the better distribution of the richness of the Church, and it would also mean the larger using of men who are deeply consecrated to the cause of Christ but who simply do not fit into the plan which the Church has at present set for herself.

Writing to the Corinthians, St. Paul said "there are diversities of gifts, but the same Spirit." The call may come quite clearly to a man, but it does not follow that he is called to preach. Parenthetically, it should be pointed out that the ministerial call is not the only call known to man. The man who is truly doing the work for which he is fitted is "called." However, when the call is definitely to the ministry its expression may still vary greatly. To quote Paul again, "God hath set some in the Church, first apostles, secondly prophets, thirdly teachers, then miracles, then gifts of healings, helps, governments, divers kinds of tongues."

In this diversity there is the unity of the vocation of the ministry itself. Many gifts, many expressions of those gifts, but one vocation.

Which leads us to the most important consideration of all. What is this vocation of the ministry? The man who confidently asserts that he has been called must also know the nature of the vocation to which he has been called. If he stated that he had been called to become a physician, or a lawyer, or an artist the world would understand. Does it understand when he says that he is called of God?

The farewell commission of Christ to His followers was that they should make disciples of all the nations, "teaching them to observe all things whatsoever I have commanded you." At the beginning of His ministry He had entered the synagogue at Nazareth, where he had been brought up, and there, on the Sabbath day, He read from Isaiah:

"The Spirit of the Lord is upon me,
  Because he anointed me to preach good tidings
      to the poor:
  He hath sent me to proclaim release to the
      captives,
  And recovering of sight to the blind,
  To set at liberty them that are bruised,
  To proclaim the acceptable year of the Lord."

He said then, "Today hath this scripture been fulfilled in your ears." His subsequent ministry developed and confirmed this statement. Then when he commissioned His disciples to carry on His work it was clear that He intended them to carry on with the same message, and with the same spirit.

Does the ministry present an easy way of achieving an education? How much mischief has the Church brought upon herself by the ready grants she has made to young men at some of our theological seminaries! There are still so many scholarships available that young men study theology who are simply there to obtain a general cultural training. If the Church should put her students on the same level as are the students of any other course, not coddling them, then she would secure a larger portion of men to lead her work, not men who are limp unless supported by the Church but men who out of the richness of their conviction and of their purpose pour contagious strength into the Church which they represent.

Does the vocation of the ministry present an easy way of making a living? The novelists of the period of Trollope picture the parish priest in England as a man of most delightful leisure who takes his religious duties as lightly as possible and who is a social favorite with the landed gentry by reason of his ready wit and his equally ready appetite. His living is always assured by

the State Church. Alas, it is one of the evils of
the State Church wherever it is that it encour-
ages a ministry which has no heart for its cause.
But State Churches are melting away in the same
measure as are crowns. Even so the Church today still has the appearance of being less strenuous than other vocations, such as finance, industry, or scientific pursuits. But the men who
enter the ministry in the hope of an easy berth
will increasingly be disillusioned. The laity is
ceasing to regard a man because of his Roman
collar and his shovel hat unless underneath those
outward symbols he is a man who carries the
burdens of his people, and strains in his agony
to bring them to things of the spirit. Even in
this generation have I seen the discard of certain
clergymen who have entered the ministry under
the mistaken lure of a soft job. With the modern
approach to religion from which the wrappings
have been ruthlessly cast aside there remains a
call to the ministry—as there was in the days of
the early Church—for men who have the courage
of their faith, and are ready to die for their convictions. We are coming upon hard days for the
Christian Church, but those hard days are of
themselves a challenge to a finer and more self-
sacrificing leadership.

The man who is called to the ministry must
have a deep sense of the evil of the world. He
must be so conscious of it that it hurts. And by
evil I mean all those divisions which keep men

and classes and nations apart. I am not thinking of those smaller conventional "sins" about which the Church has made such a fuss—dancing, cards, movies. During the World War we tried to keep our young men sober in order that they might be clean and upstanding enough to kill their "enemies" in the trenches that faced them on the battlefield. We strained at a gnat and swallowed a camel. The man who is called to be a minister must really believe that "the earth is the Lord's and the fullness thereof," and he must dedicate his life to making that truth obvious to all.

The minister is called to be the Conscience of Mankind. He will be sensitive to the evil of the world because he has a vision of what a garden of the Lord the world might be. All his thought and action, his prayer and preaching, will be directed to the supreme aim of bringing harmony out of discord, creation out of chaos. He is literally called to do the work of God in a world where the destructive forces are so powerful that the very existence of men's hardly developed communities is threatened. He must keep his eye steadily on the world-wide community where men can dwell creatively in peace.

CHAPTER TWO

TRAINING FOR THE MINISTRY

PHILLIPS BROOKS has defined the two essential
qualities for an effective ministry as culture and
consecration. No man has more completely exemplified these than did he. Without consecration a minister is as sounding brass and a tinkling
cymbal. Without culture a minister lacks the
vehicle to radiate the things of the spirit. Some
sects still have an untrained ministry, but their
impression upon this era is negligible. As a
Church emphasizes the training of her leaders so
she can expect a hearing for her message.

The influences that shape a man's life are
active long before his birth. We are growing to
value the preponderant influence of heredity.
Furthermore, the early years, when even the
most precocious child cannot escape from the influences of the home, are to be reckoned with.
How much of the unlovely, misshapen, thwarted
life is due to the associations of that life in the
home of its childhood! One would never dare
limit the operations of God's grace, yet it is almost too much to expect, even of Omnipotence,
that the product of certain homes should be well-
balanced lives whose every touch with the world

will be that of healing. The soul which normally
has the habit of thinking only, as St. Paul said in
the letter to the Philippians, of "whatsoever
things are lovely, whatsoever things are of good
report"—that soul offers the best intimations of
developing into a manhood such as is needed by
the minister of Christ. Such a condition is entirely independent of riches or poverty. The ab-
sence of this condition, however, accounts for
the presence in that elect group of men who minister the mysteries of Jesus Christ of certain
pastors to whom should never have been intrusted so exacting a vocation.

The first group of Christ's servants, upon
whom so much depended, were men of different
qualifications, but the man among them who had
the finest gifts of training became the one who
had the world vision, and who interpreted the
Gospel of Jesus Christ to every part of the world.
Paul himself, speaking to Timothy, his spiritual
son, foresaw the value of home to earlier generations when he spoke of Timothy's mother Eunice
in terms of the deepest appreciation, and even of
his grandmother Lois.

It is beyond the ability of any man to choose
his own home. The Church, however, in looking
about for candidates for her supreme office does
not dare to neglect the homes where temporal advantages abound. Every variety of equipment is
needed by the minister of God. If the Church
is to be universal in her appeal her ministry too

must be universal, with this one essential, that
from whatsoever angle it may come it must be
centered in Jesus Christ.

In the ministry the spirit and the vision of a
man come first. He must be ready to give of his
best toward the creation of a world made new
under the direction of his Lord. But he must
not face the modern world untrained. He must
be at ease in cultivated society without losing
touch with the uneducated. He cannot hope to
be a specialist in any other field than his own—
few men are today—but his general knowledge
must be more than superficial. He is to be a man
of the world in the sense that his knowledge will
be the equal of that of other men he meets in
everyday life. He must be their intellectual
equal at least, their superior if possible. And, in
the spiritual sense, he must be in the world but
not of the world.

The high intellectual ability to which the minister must aspire if he is to be worth anything to
the Church he represents brings him face to face
with the problem of the best kind of school to
attend for his training. Shall he go to a school
of his own Church or to a secular school? As one
thoroughly loyal to his Church my father had no
thought but that his sons should go to schools
of their own Church. His loyalty was so firm
that it never suffered any deviation. I have
always respected his loyalty, but such loyalty on
the part of her pastors should also be met with

a like sense of responsibility on the part of the Church.

To the eager, trusting student she has too often made answer in terms of an institution that limps in equipment and teaching force. Too late in such circumstances does the candidate discover that his training has been inadequate for the demands of his vocation. The Church also suffers from her own blindness by failing of the leadership her ministers should exercise. The candidate for the ministry is justified in asking from his Church an institution that shall give him the most complete training for his work. If she does not furnish such opportunity, is he then not entitled to seek, and will he not frequently seek, a secular institution which provides thorough training in liberal arts? In that case, as a Christian man, he will seek spiritual sustenance through the normal channels. The problem of the Church college is one of the most important links in the training for the ministry.

The Church dare not coddle or shelter her candidates for the ministry, as so often is the impulse with persons who are well intentioned but not far-sighted. The manly student will scorn such pampering, and the student who covets it has no rightful place in the ministry. The candidate must be trained to meet the world of ideas and men awaiting his ministrations after ordination. To this end he does well to rub shoulders with every variety of men during his training.

The religious teaching of the Church reaches her members through the services of the worship, through the Church school, and through the home. She has committed the sin which so easily besets us of spreading herself over areas quite beyond her resources. The Church should primarily choose the period of life that is most impressionable; here she can make her best investment. Luther four hundred years ago chose the home as the point of finest contact; and the Church of today is wise in again emphasizing the need of the family altar as the primary requisite in religious education. As she completes one stage in religious education she will be entitled to enter another.

In the early days of the life of our country it was a custom to send Lutheran young men back to Europe for their theological training. Muhlenberg did this with his three sons. Later it became the habit to have candidates live under the roof of some scholarly pastor and thus, by contact as well as by study, grow into a pastorate. This plan had so many virtues that one still looks back upon this era as producing some of the finest pastors in our American Church life. It was, however, felt to be intellectually insufficient, and the theological seminary was originated to take its place. The man gave way to the institution. A well-known student of men has said: "It is the first years after college which are the most decisive in a man's career. Any event which

happens then has its full significance. The years
which come before are too fluid; the years which
come after are too solid." And the Church in
occupying the energies of the young man during
this critical period assumes no small obligation
to the young man himself.

From the viewpoint of their obligation to the
Church these years at the seminary are beyond
estimate in their potentialities. It is a logical
conclusion that the life of the Church in the coming generation will be largely that of the students who are sent out from the seminaries. Thus
the seminary holds in its hand the future life of
the Church. Accordingly, both in its obligation
to the young men under its care and in its obligation to the Church the seminary undertakes a
contract that is not easily discharged.

In the light, however, of its high calling the
actual performance is too limited. The atmosphere of theological schools is traditionally lower
than that of other institutions. There exists a
mustiness which is associated with lack of activity.

Many earnest young men will acknowledge
that in entering the seminary their enthusiasm,
instead of being spurred on, was chilled by the
intellectual and by the spiritual standards. This
was their experience in face of the fact that on
entering a theological school from a school of
higher learning they immediately felt themselves
limited—in some instances humiliated—by the

attitude which other men of their class at college would take toward them. Their classmates as they enter their secular callings, be it business or some profession, think of themselves as entering life with a tremendous sweep, and look upon their classmates entering the theological schools for the pastoral calling with a feeling of pity. In the shadow of this attitude the candidate for the seminary suffers humiliation. To counteract this the theological seminary should immediately, at the first contact, convince the novice of the glorious work he is entering, and of the boundless life and opportunity. Tragic to relate, the life of the theological school often begins with the speed of a one-horse shay. A full test of the life of theological schools may be made by the question: How much momentum is added to the intellectual and spiritual purpose of our students during their theological training? Is it not often true that their experience robs them even of some of the ardor which was theirs when entering the seminary? The term "seminary" itself implies the idea of nursery. Does the seminary take the mental and spiritual life with gentle, patient, yet stimulating care and develop it into something strong and hardy? There are theological seminaries throughout the country that are honestly answering the challenge of the time in giving an adequate training for this exacting calling. On recent visits to my alma mater—the Lutheran Theological Seminary in

Philadelphia—I was greatly heartened to find an unfolding which did credit to this stalwart institution.

While on the subject of scholastic training for the ministry it might be well to raise the question of the value of Latin and Greek to the man who will become a minister in this modern world. His one thought is to fit himself to be an efficient instrument to convey a new spirit, a new life to men; all his training must tend toward that aim. All his studies must have that one object in view. In this light what shall we say of Latin and Greek?

It is often urged that the classics should be studied for the splendid mental training involved —an argument that might be applied with even more telling effect to Chinese! When men studied Latin in the Middle Ages they were studying not a dead but an international language. Scholars everywhere could speak in Latin, just as today diplomats of all nations communicate in French. Latin was not intellectual gymnastics; it was as essential to the educated man as English is in present-day America. It is still very much alive among the Roman Catholic priesthood and in the Catholic Church is therefore essential, not merely as an intellectual feat but for the services of the Church and for communication. If I were writing a book for Roman priests I would not raise the question of the expediency of Latin as a seminary course.

And Greek? And Hebrew?—for we must not forget Hebrew. It will be urged that without these languages the minister cuts himself off from original sources of Scripture, that he is not in a position to teach and to preach if he has little Greek and less Hebrew. This, however, is not true. The Scriptures have been translated again and again by experts, and to these expert translations the average minister can safely go. If the information he needs were available only by his studying Greek and Hebrew he would immediately study these languages. No educated man would dream of shunning Greek during the Renaissance period, when it was the door to the masterpieces of Greek literature. Today the masterpieces have been translated into English; and although the scholar still delights to read the ancient classics in the original language, the minister-to-be is not concerned with Greek as a pleasure but as a means to a practical end. If he must learn Greek it would be better to learn modern Greek, so that he can speak of Christ's new way of life to men and women whose language it is.

Although Greek and Latin were not studied in the past as mental exercises but for their practical value, there is something to be said for the mental discipline a difficult language imposes. The Russian language would provide excellent mental discipline, and when mastered would afford a potential means of communication with 168,000,-000 human beings living in the Soviet Union.

Surely it is better to be able to communicate with living, breathing human beings than with ancient books in a library! Many ministers visit Russia today—I was there myself in the winter of 1934 —and they know only too well how they are cut off from the men, women, and children they meet. If the Christian message has meaning and life in the twentieth century it has meaning and life in modern Russia, and the man who can speak that message in Russian is a man of God in the best sense of the word. He may be the world's finest classical scholar, but his knowledge will bring him no nearer the average Soviet citizen than the most uneducated American who can speak no other tongue but that which he acquired on the sidewalks of New York or Chicago. Russian would impose the severest mental discipline on the young theological student; it would also bring him near to millions of fellow human beings on this planet.

Preparation for the ministry does not end with ordination. Today is ever in preparation for tomorrow. The young minister who immediately after ordination arranges his work so that each day shall bring him new and fresh ideas will go through life with a radiance and a buoyancy that will color his entire ministry. Men are constantly facing the question whether they should work at some school even after ordination. That is in many respects a sign of better things to come. Yet every man must decide this prob-

lem for himself. Merely to add another degree
to his name is not a worthy motive, and it takes
time out of his work which really belongs to his
parish. One should closely question the subject
in which men major, whether it would not be
wiser to perfect themselves along the line of their
vocation. Contact with keen minds in school
and classroom will, however, keep a man's mind
sharp so that he can do more work in five days
than, dulled and discouraged, he might do in
seven days. It would be well for every seeker
after further training to investigate thoroughly
his own case, and possibly seek the advice of
some experienced minister.

Then there is the matter of the Church's securing great scholars who shall give their time to
writing and teaching. There is a distressing
dearth of good religious literature. Of the making of books there is no end, but to find such
literature as shall persuade the modern man of
the reality of the spiritual world is well-nigh impossible. To train such men for positions in our
theological schools the Church must constantly
be alert, taking them in their early manhood and
sparing little on their training, so that there will
always be men available for leading the religious
thought of the time. The Church is having a
supply of faithful ministers, but when one comes
to look for leaders who deservedly stand head
higher than the average pastor, then one too
often looks in vain.

CHAPTER THREE

THE SUCCESSFUL MINISTER

NOTHING is haphazard in the make-up of a successful pastor. Certain elements of character are essential to his spiritual leadership; if some are lacking he limps, if many are absent he is a burden in the Christian crusade. The sacred writers, singing the praises of the Lord of Glory, extol His strength only second to His love. The Old Testament is brimming over with allusions to His strength; in the New Testament, too, the strength of God is manifested together with the other qualities that reside in Him. In all His servants, therefore, living to build up His Kingdom, a first quality must be strength. "God hath not given us the spirit of fear but of power, of love and of a sound mind." The pastor's qualities are not merely for his own sustenance; they must brim over to enrich others.

Physical strength is a rich asset in the ministry; not only does it give intimation of moral strength, but it goes far to equip the minister for the incessant labors that are his. It is well for the minister to be employed in some occupation that will maintain his physical strength; it may be some work in the garden, or taking hikes with

his young people, or vigorous games, both in-
doors and out, which will keep his body aglow
with health. A spirit living in a healthy frame
begets the qualities needed in a successful ministry. Men have been successful without this physical foundation, but their battle is more than
half won when they enter into a situation with
the physical vigor that comes from perfect
health.

Men are increasingly making exercise a fetish
by becoming enslaved by certain rules which add
nothing to the inspiration of life and very little
to its health. The better method is to develop
this health in the pursuit of their duties. In my
early ministry, by the time I had made thirty
calls in an afternoon, which meant climbing up
many flights of stairs in tenement houses, I
needed no further exercise. Today a motorcar
is an essential of many a pastor's equipment, but
driving a car is scarcely satisfactory exercise.
The motorcar with all its gifts has robbed us of
many surprises that used to come when we
walked. If the New York pastor did more walking he would learn much about this city where
every nation of the five continents is represented.
Dr. John H. Finley, that delightful educator
through spoken and written word, walking round
the whole of Manhattan Island every birthday,
finds that his annual hike always brings him a
new story. The man who walks in our cities dis-

covers how the other half lives. And his hiking helps to bring him health!

The vigorous minister immediately offers the help that people need by his very appearance! Of course, a minister physically weak can succeed in his great errand; many have done so despite their weakness, and their unselfish immolation has brought their cause unbounded glory. Paul, the greatest Apostle, was physically defective, but he went exulting from one great task to another. It is the men who are morally weak who have no place as ministers of Jesus Christ; they bring shame to the Church. Here rests grave responsibility upon those who bring young men into the ministry. "More evil is done in the world by weak men than by wicked men." A bitter epigram but remarkably true. The man who lacks moral standards, and so disregards moral mandates, has definitely no place in the ministry. He is among the impediments of the Church; instead of ministering to others he should humbly take his place with those to be ministered to. Job says, "He that hath clean hands shall wax stronger." A man who amid toppling standards and confusing voices sees more and more clearly the difference between right and wrong—that is the man who can make a definite contribution to spiritual leadership.

There is an even greater strength, the strength that comes into the soul from God, then to be expressed in loving touch with one's fellows. The prophet Isaiah said, "They that wait upon the Lord shall renew their strength." It is when the strength of the Everlasting One becomes our strength through Word and Sacraments, through public worship and private communion, that we become fitted to be His ministers.

In addition to his strength the minister must be endowed with sympathy. This befitting a man who opens the gates of his life so that his spirit may go out and mingle in helpful relations with others. A sympathetic man shows this quality even before he confesses to it. He is so sensitive to the condition of his fellows that he cannot but rejoice with those that rejoice, and weep with those that weep. This is totally alien to the thoroughly selfish man. Its most successful expression is in the man who forgets himself. He enters into the joys and sorrows of others as though they were his own. The spirit of such a man runs before him, gaining him an entrance before he arrives! Successful ministers always have been beloved of children. Martin Luther had his happiest experiences when singing with his children.

A lady describing the last Sunday morning in the life of Phillips Brooks—recorded in *Life and Letters of Phillips Brooks* by Alexander V. G. Allen—reveals the happy relationship of the great minister with children:

"After the confirmation he stayed and

stayed," this lady stated. "I have never seen him happier or gentler, never more childlike and lovable than he was that Sunday morning. He addressed the Sunday-school. When that was done he went about among the children. Women brought him their babies and their boys that he might look into their faces. He had a word for every one. When he sat down, a group of boys circled around him. One boy back of him noticed a speck upon his coat and went to brush it off. In a moment there were three boys brushing him all together. He looked about and colored, his modesty overcome at being the object of so much attention. . . . He continued to talk with the children. It seemed even then that he was already entering God's kingdom as a little child."

The sympathy without which no minister is truly a minister is often exploited. Cranks, bores, fanatics, the shiftless, fasten upon him, draining his strength if he seeks no measure of self-protection. Some New York clergymen are so well protected that visitors reach them only by card after a secretary's scrutiny. Ministers who shun this procedure as un-Christlike—Jesus moved freely in the open air, unprotected by secretaries—find such demands made upon their time that they are constantly interrupted. Jesus mingling in a dense crowd perceived that power had gone forth from Him when the woman touching the hem of His garment was healed of her issue of blood. No "protection" there! And yet that same Jesus, so approachable that men, women, and children came to Him without fear, also withdrew Himself on occasion. "Come ye yourselves apart into a desert place, and rest a while," He said. He recognized that even the most self-giving of men must be alone at times. If they would be strong to help they must seek strength in retreat.

The ministers who survive the strain of living in New York are those who organize their time. They can attempt to live in the spirit of Jesus, but they cannot model their daily life upon His. Even if we knew much more of His daily life it would not serve as the regular routine of the modern minister. What a separation there is between the pastoral Palestine of the first century and the mechanical America of today! The minister who would follow his Lord must do so in the spirit, not in the letter. He must use his own judgment as to the best expenditure of time and energy in his twenty-four-hour day. If he is a preacher he must concentrate on preaching, leaving the bulk of pastoral work to another man, coöperating in the work of his church with him whose gifts as a pastor are greater than his gifts as a preacher. However, the preacher is sometimes pastor, the pastor sometimes preacher. Even in an age of specialization the minister must avoid overspecialization. One brilliant New York preacher devotes his afternoons to seeing people in his study, hearing their problems, sympathetically leading them out of their troubles. He keeps in touch with the world of men, he gains an insight into their lives, invaluable for his preaching; and he is not torn to pieces spiritually as he would be if he were carrying other people's burdens without respite.

In the early days of the depression so many men and women who had lost their money, or their jobs, or both, came to ministers of the Church for material and spiritual help that even the most sympathetic of men found the task of helping them far beyond their spiritual strength and their financial means. They had to form committees, bring in assistants, introduce some "red tape." Unsympathetic? Sometimes, perhaps; as a rule, no. They were ordinary men overwhelmed by an extraordinary calamity. Many of them had never questioned the "permanent prosperity" of the social system under which they lived. When they discovered that modern society—finance, industry, business—is like a leaky boat on a high sea they frantically did their best to help their people, and many other persons who had not been near a church in a long time. If ministers did not reveal themselves as experts in this new task they at least found that the supposed experts—statesmen, politicians, the kings of finance, captains of industry, big businessmen—were just as much at sea as they were. With the best of intentions they could not solve all the economic problems of

the day in addition to the new spiritual problems
with which they were confronted. The Church
like Martha became "cumbered with much serving" in a crisis which seemed to demand just
that. The prayer and meditation of a Mary
seemed out of touch with the times when men,
women, and children were clamoring for food to
eat, clothes to wear, shelters in which to sleep.
Christ Himself fed the hungry, and He recognized the place of food in our lives when He included the petition "Give us this day our daily
bread" in His own prayer. Man cannot live by
bread alone, but without bread he dies. A double
problem which the Church can never avoid while
she ministers to mortal men. The successful minister is the man who knows how to create a balance between the material and the spiritual, not
confusing the one with the other, not permitting
either to go beyond its own domain. Is that impossible? Not in a world where men are both
bodies and spirits. The perpetual miracle of life
on this planet is the keeping of bodies and souls
together in something like 2,000,000,000 human
beings. Man is not pure spirit, neither is he mere
matter. The Church ministers to a miraculous
combination of spirit and matter.

The minister, from the very nature of his work,
leads a life that is separate from ordinary avenues. The fault which the layman finds with
many sermons is that they do not relate to his
daily life. For this reason the minister must

make a special effort to put himself forth so as to be in touch with the daily life of his men. He must know the hardships they endure in their efforts to support their families. He must know the difficulty of keeping straight in business. It is well for him to indulge in their sports. These things the minister must do because so much of his vocation emphasizes the gentler side of life; without these activities he will be respected by the men but he will not be trusted as one who is able to help them. The minister who is completely sympathetic with men will see the masculine side of the congregation grow because he understands their language and knows their problems.

The Protestant Church must ever be grateful to Martin Luther for having courageously instituted the Protestant parsonage. Society must be indebted to him because out of the parsonage there still comes a large number of the leaders of this country. In the 1934-35 edition of Who's Who in America, from a list of eighteen occupations the sons of ministers lead by a wide margin, having 11 per cent of the entrants. The family is the normal relation in which a man is to live; why, therefore, should not the minister be married? The wife of the minister is often as much of a help in the conduct of the parish as the minister himself. I have often thought of the shrewdness of congregations in paying a mediocre salary and thereby obtaining two trained workers. This double service again shows that the ideal of the Christian ministry is service. The minister does not reckon himself as receiving a quid pro quo; he wholeheartedly, with his wife, throws himself into the development of the lives of the people, and therefrom receives enough to live by with thrift.

There is, however, much to be said for the Roman Catholic ideal of the priest living a celibate life, throwing himself untrammeled by family cares into the service of the Church. Much heroic adventure has been undertaken by priests and ministers who are free from the distractions and responsibilities of home life. Every Church body should have at its call some men who are free to come and go as occasion arises.

The successful minister must be a man of joy. I have seen young men enter the ministry who would succeed only by a special endowment of grace, so somber was their mien. The long-faced minister may have been more successful at certain periods, but he will not succeed in this present era, when conditions are more exacting on the minister. His temperament must be joyous, with a joy born of faith. The letters of St. Paul are brimming over with joy, and that in the face of discouragements and hardships which no minister today experiences. That joy had in it an element of buoyancy which was contagious, bearing him up when there were a number of weights that would otherwise have brought him to earth. The minister must not let the cares of his present parish embitter him. His people and his field must be the most attractive to him; if they are not it is his privilege to make them so. My first parish, which started out as a mission parish, became so attractive that to my mind it seemed the only place where I should spend my life. Men about me were called to other places, but I loved the people too well ever to consider that other places might have advantages. It was only after twelve years that at the command of the Church I finally left to undertake what the Church deemed a wider work, that of a student pastorate at the universities of Columbia, Cornell, Yale, Harvard, and Syracuse.

The greatest preachers of the world have been poets. In this they have but followed the Supreme Teacher, Christ Himself. Not only He but all of our sacred literature constantly turns to poetry because there is no other message to express the sublime mysteries of grace. In recent years this has been exemplified by those masters of the pulpit in New York, John Henry Jowett, of the Fifth Avenue Presbyterian Church, and Robert Norwood, of St. Bartholomew's Episcopal Church. The successful minister must therefore use and strengthen his imagination. If this is not found among his "cradle gifts" he must develop it in his thinking and by his reading. It is distressing that no more use of this faculty is made in the preparation for the ministry. I would recommend most earnestly the study of Dr. John Kelman's article on "Poetry" in Hastings' Dictionary of Christ and the Gospels. It ends with this climax: "That ideal world, so far ahead of the most spiritual of us all, yet so persistently claiming us as its children, and beckoning us to the courageous renewal of our broken attempts to reach it, is a world which could have been constructed for man only by God incarnate in One who was a poet."

This faculty of forming images differentiates the effective preacher from the one who lives only in his earthbound thoughts. Imagination brightens the path of our dreary sermons and peoples them with the bright forms of spirits who are led by the voice of the Eternal. Imagination finds in Holy Writ oases and bulwarks for the believer which become more precious to him than "the treasure which moth and dust corrupt and thieves break through and steal." Imagination gives purpose to our work—oh, how needed! —and finds in the mind of Christ His plan for the individual, the family, the State, and the world, and then without haste but without rest tries to achieve it because it is the plan of Christ.

That minister only is successful who is filled with the spirit of God, and the fruit of that spirit is "love, joy, peace, longsuffering, gentleness, goodness, faithfulness, meekness, temperance."

CHAPTER FOUR

THE SINS OF THE MINISTER

PAUL, in his letter to the Hebrews, warns against "the sin that doth so easily beset us." This statement always brings to me the picture of someone lurking around the corner, awaiting an opportunity to enter the house when no one is on the alert. There are sins lurking around the corner of a pastor's life, seeking to gain entrance and to prey upon him. He is subject to the entire gamut of human temptation; in addition he is haunted by special sins ever ready to destroy him.

The minister's ordination gives him no special character. He must grapple with the temptations he shares with his flock. He will grow into strength and Christian manhood only as he battles with the sins that would tear him down. The man in the pew often thinks of the minister as being removed from all such ensnaring temptations, and rarely gives him credit for the fight he must wage all his days if he would maintain a life that is blameless before God and man.

One of the minister's special sins arises from the conditions of his work. He is not a laborer digging a ditch with a foreman over him, crack-

ing the whip, figuratively speaking, if he shows
signs of slowing up! The minister has no such
taskmaster. He retires to his "cloister," and it
may be years before his congregation knows the
quality of the work done every morning in that
retreat. Whether he prays and studies and reads
in sincerity is a matter between him and his un-
seen Master. Not immediately will anyone de-
tect either flabbiness or hardness of mind and
heart born of the way he has spent the time on
many mornings in that upper room. He may
daydream in his easy-chair. The Church Board
will not be there to chide him. Instead of prim-
ing his mind with helpful and living thoughts to
be given to his people he may find it much easier
to abandon the task, and to borrow from some
master of the past. All this, and much more, can
he do in the misuse of a quiet period in his
"cloister," and the tragic part of it is that the result of such indolence does not soon rise to the
surface.

The minister is tempted to be idle. He may
form the habit of indolence, a habit which, once
formed, will fasten hard upon him. It comes si-
lently, an insidious intruder. It is like a drug
under the spell of which the victim loses his
sense of responsibility. The meaning of the word
"indolence" shows it to be applicable to the person who ceases to grieve. Not only cares but
duties slip away from him. The strength of his

personality is sapped. He no longer counts in God's world.

On one of my visits to Berlin I went through the palace of the Crown Prince on Unter den Linden, where one is shown the high desk at which the first Emperor stood as he worked. What a protection against the lure of the all-too-easy chair! The minister who is tempted to laziness would be wise to try the experiment of standing at a high desk. He should certainly banish the easy-chair from his study. Even for quiet reading it is more conducive to somnolence than to thought. The easy-chair has its uses for relaxation in the living-room, not for work in the study.

The minister who never goes into his study finds ways of wasting his time comparable to the laziness of the man who sleeps in his chair. He loves to hang about the garage and the post office and other public places of his community. True, he can say that he is establishing contact with the human life around him; but the man who never studies, never thinks, never enters the "cloister," has nothing to contribute to that life. He sinks to the level of the loafer. He has no word of inspiration to bring, no message to startle people who seem beyond the possibility of startling.

The minister's pastime may become another form of indolence. It is fine to have an avocation, but when a man allows his avocation to become his vocation tragedy lies ahead. The introduction of multigraphs into parish work is thought to be a distinct step forward, but some ministers devote so much time to the multigraphing of announcements of services and sermons that they have no opportunity to prepare for those occasions! Taking care of an automobile or cultivating a garden is not only legitimate but, in the case of a garden, quite charming. But neither avocation should claim the principal interest in a minister's life. Paul tells Timothy to give himself "wholly" to his pastoral duties. It is always surprising that the Church succeeds as well as she does when her pastors are so divided in the allegiance they give her.

The radio has revolutionized public speech. The speaker must begin and end at the exact moment. He must know precisely what he wishes to say, and he must say it within a given time. How fortunate his congregation would be if every preacher gave his sermon under conditions approximating the radio program! Slovenliness of thought and expression would come near being banished. Precision would be forced upon the preacher, otherwise he would lose out completely. He would be compelled to spend fruitful hours in his study. He would come to realize the necessity of having something to say, and of saying it clearly.

This precision would enter the full program of his pastoral activities. The Church, through her pastors, would register more strokes that really count. It is stimulating to think back upon some of the men of God who have made history, and to note how crowded their lives were with things that counted. Paul, in addition to preaching in all parts of the then known world and writing literature that is among the finest, had daily, beyond these activities, the care of all the churches. Martin Luther was constant in his teaching and preaching, in addition to which he did the work of many men in writing volumes upon various phases of the Christian life, besides being called upon all the time to guide the new Reformation movement. Moreover, he performed the almost superhuman task of translating the Old and New Testaments into the language of the German people. The example of men such as these must make the average pastor ashamed of his own attainments and must stimulate him to make his life count in the greatest of all professions. Jesus was weary after His day's work. Dare any pastor expect to be less weary?

Formalism is a sin that so readily besets the minister; it is indolence in another form. He is content to practice the forms of religion and to perform ceremonies without putting into them the soul without which the forms are dead. In the expression of all kinds of religion this is the besetting sin. It is being content with the outward sign when the soul is absent. How to fill the form of our words and worship with spiritual food for the souls of hungry men and women is a problem that should be faced more frequently than it is.

Generation after generation goes on saying the same words without pausing to ask whether they are freighted with human desires and needs. It is strange that we should be content with forms that mean so little and at the same time expect the grace of an omnipotent and loving Father to come into our lives through them. We lose God-given institutions in formalism. Antireligious activities in the Soviet Union gain their force and significance from the failure of the Church to give spiritual values to forms which, when empty, count for nothing vital in the experience of the people. In the same way, pastoral visitation, which should provide vital contact for pastor and people, will have no meaning if undertaken as a matter of form, or to enable the pastor to report so many calls to his Church Board and Synodical officials.

Paul, that veteran pastor, writing to his spiritual son, Timothy, warns him against being a novice, "lest being lifted up with pride he fall into the condemnation of the devil." Possibly self-conceit is the special sin of young men, but it seems to me that it confronts the pastor throughout his life, always trying to enter. The sin of pride is a peculiar temptation to the minister. He is normally the head of the parish; his word is law. Those who disagree with his policy are

either discarded or they cease to take interest in
what he is doing. Fresh from the seminary, a
man set apart, with a large number of the women
of the church worshiping a Roman collar—it is
difficult for a young man to maintain a humble
spirit. Whatever is done in the parish redounds
to the credit of the minister, often unjustly. I
have frequently observed the rise of a young man
to success with a feeling of positive sorrow as I
have seen his pride in his own powers get the
better of him. Humility is one of the most beautiful flowers in the garden of virtue. Every pastor must strive valiantly that he keep under his
self-conceit, which would destroy one of the most
outstanding virtues of a Christian. Self-conceit,
little by little, cuts him off from his brethren,
whose fellowship would otherwise be a constant
refreshment to him. He becomes impatient with
the poor, unlike Brother Lawrence, who said
when he brought the poor of his parish to the
Emperor, "These are my treasures." More tragic
than anything else is the fact that he cuts off that
current of divine grace which makes a pastorate
effective. St. Paul said, "When I am weak, then
am I strong."

The test of a minister's character is largely
shown by his relationship with his fellow ministers. He may fare well with his congregation,
where he occupies a unique position, but when he
becomes one of a group, then sometimes ugly
forms appear from the windows of his soul.

Forms of envy, jealousy, lack of charity. One way to estimate the character of a man is to find out how he judges his predecessor in a parish. It is good if he speaks well of the former pastor. If he discounts everything that his predecessor has done, then he reveals himself to be, despite his sacred office, no finer than the man who makes no profession of being a Christian. In the German language there is a word *Schadenfreude,* meaning "joy at the evil which befalls others." This is too often found in the hearts of our pastors with reference to their fellow pastors. It indicates a lack of interest in the work of the Kingdom of God and goes far to paint the picture of the pastor as being interested only in his own advancement. The laymen in our congregations are constantly a source of surprise and joy; they see the failings of the pastor, but, with a spirit of charity that the pastor might well emulate, they cover up his sins.

Preaching is truth through personality. For nineteen centuries the truth of Christ has been preached, and if a man is true to himself he will present a facet of that truth never before presented. Every man has his peculiar gifts through which the truth is proclaimed. Every preacher, therefore, should present a distinct facet of the truth. When indolence leads to his saying what other men have said before him he loses the charm and the conviction which should flow from a man giving expression to the truth within him. Ministers fail to capture the interest and stimulate the minds of their congregations when they repeat threadbare words instead of presenting the truth given to them. They lose the joy of freshness; their words are like trodden flowers beneath the feet of passers-by. If only they would learn the joy of being themselves in their ministry, what strength they would bring to their parish and pulpit!

Albert Einstein, on the occasion of his receiving the medal of the Franklin Institute, merely smiled his thanks when scores of scientists from Philadelphia and the vicinity, assembled to hear him speak on "Physics and Reality," eagerly awaited some startling pronouncement. Quite frankly he explained that he had nothing to say at that moment, hence there was no alternative save silence. I sometimes feel that the preacher might well follow the example of this great scientist and if he found, some Sunday, he had no message, would refrain from entering his pulpit. A service for worship would feed the congregation more effectively than the addition of a sermon which pastor and people would realize had been inserted simply because it was a traditional part of the service. A sermon omitted at times would create a deeper impression among people than the regularity of sermons delivered in season and out of season.

All the sins of the minister finally resolve themselves into this defect, that he is not constantly living in the presence of Christ. The Master defined sin as not believing on Him. When one analyzes the failure of the message one eventually finds some defect in the pastor's relationship with his Lord and Master. With this relationship as the primary requisite, the life of every minister ought to grow richer year by year in the things of the spirit. In the growth of this there will be a joy, lacking in so many lives, and it will make a minister so effective that new joys will follow.

The minister is to be a minister all the time. He is not to be a minister for certain days and certain hours of the day only. Filled with a passion for people, he will be helpful whenever the opportunity arises, whether in his immediate parish or outside its bounds. In fact, he can sometimes be of more value to some seeker after truth if he meets him on the equal plane of travel, business, or recreation. Words have value when uttered in such surroundings as against the conventional elevation of the pulpit. It is said of St. Francis of Assisi that he was a current benediction. How the spiritual atmosphere of the world would rise if of each one to whom has been given the gifts of ordination a like characterization could be made!

One of America's brightest young business men lamented to me that ministers are seldom willing to speak on subjects concerning which they should be specialists. He wanted not a

formal discourse from the pulpit, in which he
could take no part, but an opportunity to ask
questions as man to man, so that they might open
themselves to the great things of the spirit. To
such a man the pulpit is aggravating because it
seems unreal. It smacks of the Pharisee, both
in its formality and in its holier-than-thou attitude. This is quite different from the method
of the Master; He did His most effective work
with individuals. He thus enlisted all His disciples, held His midnight conversations with
Nicodemus, tested the Rich Young Ruler, and
left us the priceless gem of the quiet home in
Bethany. To the servant of Christ such opportunities are coming today with increasing fre-
quency, and response to them can be made more
effective than a routine sermon.

CHAPTER FIVE

THE QUIET PERIOD

COMING toward the end of his life, the great Apostle Paul wrote Timothy, "I thank Jesus Christ, our Lord, who hath enabled me, for that he counted me faithful, putting me into the ministry." This definite giving of thanks was made despite perils and hostilities which he had already faced, and the imprisonment which, he realized, was ahead of him. Paul's gratitude for his holy calling did not, therefore, depend upon the comfort of his position.

I regret to say that most of the pious expressions of joy in the ministry come from a satisfaction with outward things. There is a beautiful and complete church equipment, a cultured congregation, the mutual flattery on the part of congregation and pastor, so agreeable to both, and one is distressed to find so little consciousness of the service of the lowly Nazarene. A leader in a sister church recently, in a popular magazine, gave the attractions of the ministry, and there was not one but would make a sincere servant of Christ blush for shame. During these days of Church strife in Germany there are evidences of pastors fighting through their battle on purely spiritual lines. The material is swept away from under their feet, yet despite that they claim spiritual experiences the like of which they had never known in the days of calm and outward peace. If the Church should secure her strength from such a reservoir she would more effectively command the interest of the world.

I would ask the minister of the future to have the same joy in his ministry as Paul, although he will face obstacles as difficult as his. It is well to face the fact that a young man going out into the ministry today is confronted by a world that has completely changed during the past generation. Instead of standing for regimented life consisting of so many weeks with a Sunday to be observed each week, and that usually by going to church, this series of standards has absolutely faded out. So many things have recently come into life, claiming prior interest, that the ancient landmarks have been washed away. The tirade from the pulpit against motoring and other recreations on Sunday has become so worn-out that it is rarely attempted. Some communities have tried to buttress Sunday observance by the enactment, and by the rediscovery, of rigid Blue Laws. These buttresses to religion are gradually being disintegrated by the will of the people. In our modern industrial life, Sunday stands more as the center of a weekend than it does as the day for the promulgation of God's will and the conferring of His grace. In former generations

Sunday brought the atmosphere of the Church and even to the most rebellious it still brought a tugging of conscience. Today the current flows in the opposite direction. Instead of being a marked man for not attending to his religious duties, he is a marked man who does. The former social obligation to the Church has disappeared before a generation that sees no obligation to religion. The generation that is now arising has taken to itself a pragmatic attitude—unless an institution can prove its worth it will not be adopted. In former years the Church stood in the community with an attitude that was defiant toward many who were not interested in her. That defiance has today passed into a pathetic harmlessness. Religion can be chosen as life's avocation as one would choose music or art, but there is no universal claim coming from the pulpit.

In addition to this, the Church as an institution has become so distressingly mixed up with secularism for her support that the minds of many of the most devout people are turned away from her for this reason. The various methods of chance or vaudeville entertainment that even the legitimate theater would not stand are being used to support an anaemic and often dying institution. It is not surprising that people of the finest motive refuse to be drawn into such a maze. These things are often done because Church Boards claim they hold the young people. On the contrary, however, they drive away many young people who are seeking a serious institution through which to express themselves.

These are some of the problems which the young man going out into the world as an ambassador of Christ must face in the organized Church of today. Our fathers did not know them; to us they are almost insuperable problems, and they will require consecration greater than that of the past generation if we are to remain loyal to Christ and His ideals. The present generation also requires of us an extension of our work. We have been apt to fall back in a protective sense on the fact that our obligation was simply to the individual. More and more is thrust upon us the social obligation which must be the result of an individual religion. However, the prophet of the present day must help in guiding the intentions of his people. When one realizes the present state of the world with its selfish nationalism, with nations uncovering their real motives, one feels the lack of love in the councils of the world. This is due, largely, to the fact that Christian pastors have not sufficiently promulgated the need of Christian love. In times of war, the pulpit becomes excited in striving to engender hatred of the enemy. In the interregnum, between wars, the Christian pastor thinks too little of the obligation which each of his people has in creating a brotherhood of the people of the world. We are confronted with such disastrous spectacles both in national and in international affairs that the Church must vitally propose a substitute for this method of treating our fellows who are of different color or on the other side of the globe. This part of his message will mean an added problem to the minister of the coming age, but it is a contribution which he dare not pass by if he would be a faithful minister of Jesus Christ.

We felt in former days the stability of existing institutions. Church and State and family, as we knew them, were as unchangeable as the hills. Today, there is no one who is not uncertain as to the future of these institutions. By evolution or by revolution each of them, or all, may undergo a complete change. Still, it will be the function of the Christian minister to continue in loyalty to Christ and proclaim the Gospel. I veritably believe the coming generations will disentangle us from the maze into which we have fallen, and that those who have the persistence will stand out more clearly as ambassadors of Jesus Christ.

What then is the function of the minister of Jesus Christ when many of the buttresses that have supported his work, false or true, have disappeared? Martin Niemöller, a leader in Germany's struggle for a spiritual church, gave me during my visit at his parsonage in Berlin, a copy of his fast-selling *From U Boat to Pulpit*. On the flyleaf he wrote these lines, "To hear a word, a command that shall direct and control all your days—this is life." This should be the purpose of every pastor, by word and life so to express the Eternal Word of Jesus Christ that it will create in the spirit of man that magnet from which he can never escape.

The problem that must then confront the young man going out to create such a magnet must be: How can I resolve myself into such a minister? "He who would pour water must first draw it" is a proverb that has well proved itself. In the attractive story of the home of Bethany our Lord clearly points the way when He tells Martha, the sister who is busy with much serving, "One thing is needful and Mary hath chosen the good part which shall not be taken away from her." So to the minister one thing is preëminently needful; other things are merely relatively so. If his ministry is to go on from strength to strength, with constantly greater joy and gratitude for his having been called to that vocation, then he must observe this one thing needful. Too many ministers, when they come to the time which should prove their great usefulness, have shriveled up spiritually; and they spend the rest of their lives in unhappy criticism of the Church which gives them no further opportunities.

The minister's ever present temptation is to be doing something. He thus best satisfies his own conscience; he also gives the impression to his congregation of being busy in his calling. The young missionary going out to build up his congregation is always encouraged to be tireless in visiting the homes of the community. The larger the number of people he comes to know and to call by name, the more successful is he thought to be. It is the repetition of Martha's activity when she was troubled about many things; but neither the members of his congregation nor the young pastor's superiors in office ever question him as to his Lord Jesus Christ. This is that peculiar tendency in our lives where first things are forgotten in our interest in secondary things. Nowhere is this so evident as in the Church; therefore the pastor must almost forcibly take hold of himself and dedicate the mornings of his weekdays to prayer and preparation in the quietness of his study. This room in the pastor's home should not be the most public room, but should be retired, somewhat like a cloister. Every caller at the parsonage should not be breaking in upon the pastor's time and thought. After my first pastorate in Brooklyn had become organized I secured a house which had on its top floor a bright studiolike room, from the inviting windows of which I could look out upon the sky without being disturbed by the sights of the street. When I wanted a rest or a change in the course of my work I could get up and look through a wide window, or a rather fascinating porthole high in the wall beside my desk. This was my "cloister," where I could pray and think

and write in the midst of a very busy life.   In too
many pastors' homes the study is made the most
public part of the house. Nobody comes into that
family but through this so-called sanctum. Men-
dicants, tradesmen, book agents—everybody is
immediately ushered into that room, which is
about as private as a department-store window.
Every telephone call must be made and answered
in the pastor's study. The procession of events
and persons which marches through this study is
practically sufficient to take up the entire morning in the pastor's life. What, then, becomes of
his quiet period? A change of study to some
secluded part of the house will release a large
portion of his time for his distinctive needs. It
is better to have an attic on the third floor than a
drawing-room on the first floor. Such a retreat
should have prominently in its furnishings some
picture of Christ, such as "The Tribute Money"
by Titian, or an appealing statue, such as Thor-
waldsen's Christ; under all conditions it should
be a work of art that has meant something in the
pastor's own experience and so speaks a repeated
message each time he enters into its presence. It
helps to realize Christ as definitely present.
Charles E. Jefferson in his volume of studies in
the life of the Apostle Paul acknowledged that he
knew Paul better than he knew any contempo-
rary living man. What vital men our pastors
would come to be if each one might say the same
of the One Whom he calls Lord.

Then comes that meditation or brooding over the Word of God! Happy is the man who in his own devotion seeks until he finds the things hidden in that Book of Books. The temptation for the pastor always is to be looking for texts; he should, therefore, read the Word of God to his own spiritual culture and strengthening. We are having more and more books of devotion coming out in the Church. Many of these are helpful and many of them are but short cuts to devotion. It is better that a pastor should brood over a verse in the original, and then out of this discover nuggets of gold which will mean much more to him than anything prepared by some other man. The joy that comes from discovering for oneself some new truth goes far beyond the satisfaction of having a mass of information that other men have gathered. The exercise of meditation is not only a passive process. It is not daydreaming in a comfortable chair and finally falling asleep. It is the active taking-hold of some great thought and holding on to that with tenacity, until new facets of the original thought present themselves. It is keeping on the road without knowing where the road will end. It is being subject to some great conception and living with it until it speaks. It is far from being simply passive; it should be logically the most active thing in our whole day's occupation.

Just as the period of meditation is to be a definite one in the pastor's daily program, so must be the time of prayer. Anselm said, "Read until you are tempted to pray." It is the logical thing that God speaks first to men. This in turn, with absolute logic, should then inspire men to speak to God. Men can have definite periods for these spiritual exercises. The call to the minister is, therefore, that they be given place among the first demands on his time.

In these times the faithful minister will think of the problems of his parish and of individuals. He will intercede for them and he will project them into the light of Christ, in Whose light they will be transfigured, and problems that before seemed insoluble will yield themselves to the minister's tact and wisdom.

Of course there are always good books, new and old, in that study, which give evidence of having been read. There are not only books of theology and church management, but there will be volumes on nature, science, history, and especially of biography. The culture that is available to every man who keeps his mind open to opportunities for reading is beyond anyone's reckoning. Reading, however, must not simply go along the lines of one's pleasure, but should often take hold of that which is difficult to grasp. The late Sir William Robertson Nichol, famous editor of the *British Weekly*, tells how each day he would give a period to wrestling with reading. The only way to develop one's mind is in day by day attempting that which is not easily within reach.

The runner does not complete his marathon the first day he attempts it. He reaches the goal by successive days of running. So does the pastor accomplish clear thought and the ability to battle with philosophies of life only by dwelling each day upon some of the more difficult problems of life. They need not have their regular daily schedule, but they are much more certain of a hearing in the busy pastor's life if, day by day, they are admitted when the hour strikes.

Modern life may bring the minister new tasks. The organization of our churches may suffer a complete change, but behind all change he is ever essentially the ambassador of Christ. To his soul must come the ministry of the spirit before he can administer of the spirit to others. He must take in before he can give out. That is the secret of the Master's message to Mary and Martha.

CHAPTER SIX

THE PASTOR AND HIS PEOPLE

THERE are two basic requisites for every minister. He must know the love of Christ and he must be animated by love of his people. Any young man who is without either of these two qualifications would better plan his life along some other direction. A minister must be genuinely eager to help those among whom his lot has been cast. He can sometimes develop this quality. St. Francis lived with lepers so that he might come to love all men. A candidate for the ministry should try himself out before he enters the sacred office. If human beings do not attract him, and if he does not rejoice with those that rejoice and weep with those that weep, he can scarcely look forward to a happy lifework. A minister is not to be a driver, he is to be a coworker with his people, leading them in the work that they are to do and the sacrifices they are to bring. He is not to be a flatterer, indulging in one of the most despicable practices to gain the favor of his people. They will soon discover his lack of sincerity. He is not to have the slap-on-the-back attitude which is practiced in so many modern circles. He will have respect for each man's personality and recognize the dignity that resides in each human soul. The minister can

best draw the people to himself by gaining their
affection, and affection is best gained by showing
that affection has gone out from the pastor to his
people. This is revealed by a concern in the entire gamut of their existence. The pastor is to
be a father in God whose interests are not only
in the spiritual state but also in the temporal
problems with which everyone must contend.

In the generation that was represented by my
father's ministry, this attitude was a natural one.
In his pastorate of almost fifty years, my father's
relation to his parish was certainly the fatherly
one. Men would come to consult him with reference to their material problems, and, a man of
wide experience, he could usually advise them
as to the best conduct of a farm or merchandise.
In these days of big business a minister would
scarcely be expected to be able to guide the temporal affairs of his flock. He can, however, be
very much interested in the development of his
young people, with whom he should have the
most vital and sympathetic relation. He should
advise the most gifted among them to continue
their studies and prepare themselves for some position of leadership, and everyone should be stim-
ulated by him to prepare themselves to the fullest
for any eventuality that life may bring them. He
should suggest attractive books to read, and
know the very best of drama and music so that
he may enter sympathetically into each department of life. This will beget a greater love of

mankind and will prove to his people that he is sincerely interested in their pursuits.

As the more severe trials of life come among his people, he will be able to show the sincerity of his love for them. In sickness and in death a tactful pastor can bind his people to himself with bonds of steel. The primary avenue whereby a minister comes to prove his love for his people lies in the simple method of calling upon his people. This should normally occupy the pastor's afternoons, as the quiet period in his study should occupy his mornings. There is no better way to keep in touch with the people of the parish than by going to see them in their homes. Other methods have been tried and they have been found wanting. Some of the most faithful pastors make calls during the year in numbers that make one gasp. The result is, however, that they always have the love of their people. What more precious treasure can any pastor possess?

The minister can best gain the confidence of his people by showing himself worthy of such confidence. The frivolous, jesting man who has no sense of the dignity or the sacredness of his calling will never get the confidence of his people. They may enjoy his jests and they may value his entertaining powers, but as for being a man in whom they can trust, that is not the fortune of such a one. When a pastor has gained the affection and the confidence of the people, then is he able to lead them and they will gladly follow.

However, not until he has secured these two relations should a pastor ever undertake new programs in his church. And then he should deal patiently with his people. Many a relationship between pastor and people has been wrecked by a lack of patience on the part of the pastor. St. John addresses the recipients of his letters as little children, showing his degree of patience. Our Lord had been with His disciples for three years, intimately, an intimacy more than any modern pastor can cultivate with his congregation. At the end of that time, instead of being interested in the things of the Kingdom of God, the three most advanced disciples are quibbling among themselves as to who should be the greatest. It saddened the Master, but He Who knew what was in men knew that He could expect nothing more. So must it be with the tactful minister. But the attachment of the people to the minister is not the final purpose of a minister's life. In too many instances this seems to be the goal. Congregations make idols of their pastors, they make rich gifts to them. They send them abroad on holidays, and the height of success seems to be attained when such a mutual relationship has been developed between the pastor and the people.

This is the method of the so-called popular minister who has succeeded when he has secured the loyalty of a large group of people. Such a congregation and its minister indulge themselves in a vicious circle. Every effort of the congre-

gation rests upon itself and the minister feeds
the hearts of the people with honeyed words of
praise. When the leader of such a flock leaves or
dies, the congregation collapses. Its success may
have been startling in the eyes of the community,
but to more sober judgment it is but the indul-
gence of a selfish man, who, accordingly, makes
his congregation selfish. The minister must lead
his congregation higher than himself. He must
be animated by the spirit of Christ, and deeds of
love must be performed in the parish to those
who are in need of them. In many of our cities
the church stands on an island with multitudes
of unchurched people about it; the congregation
comes from the suburbs. The minister to the
church needs to be concerned with the souls of
people who live near to the church property irrespective of their color or their social condition.

The parish should make itself felt in the lives
of its neighbors, and then with a passion that
cannot be changed continue outward in blessing
until it reaches the ends of the community. That
is the secret of a successful pastorate. What a
joy it is to have a people so attuned to the needs
of men and to the purpose of Christ that like a
great orchestra the minister directs the operations of his parish, and the result of it is a symphony of beauty and goodness that elevates men
and that brings glory to Christ.

Young men are apt to recoil from the taking
of certain work because of the conditions of the

parish. The consecrated man enters the parish attracted not by what he finds at the time of his entry, but by the possibilities he sees; and year after year he enters into them. This kind of man finds joy in his work not by reason of any éclat that may come to him, but by reason of lives that have been changed, of visions that have been enlarged, and of gifts that before have been hidden.

The wise minister adds to his resources a constantly increasing number of leaders from among his own people. One of the most successful pastorates with which I have been in touch for many years was that at the Church of the Reformation in Rochester, of the Rev. Dr. Franklin F. Fry. Had he done nothing else but develop a splendid group of adjutants his work would have blessed not only his parish but the Church throughout the world. Whatever time is spent by a pastor in the training of leaders will be wisely used. There is nothing that makes his messages from the pulpit so effective as the examples of men and women who have counted in the work of Christ. The Church should have more biographies, and its shelves should be filled especially with the stories of consecrated men and women. There are ministers who do their work singlehanded, but they either fail or break down completely. There are others who multiply themselves by creating a contagious spirit in the lives of those who trust them. That is the privilege of leadership, and it is one of the joys of the ministry.

CHAPTER SEVEN

THE PASTOR AS MAN OF THE WORLD

THE title of this chapter may suggest several directions of thought. I love to think of it, however, as giving the pastor such a position in the world that everything that takes place is of interest to him. The late Archbishop Soderblom, of Sweden, was a splendid example of the man of the world. I had come to know him while he was professor at Leipzig in 1913, and had seen him at the First Lutheran World Convention at Eisenach in 1923; but in 1934 I had the privilege of being guest in the archiepiscopal palace in Upsala for a week. It was there that I first came to value thoroughly his remarkable versatility. Not only did he speak fluently the languages of Europe and America but also he knew the development of thought, not only ecclesiastical but political, in each of these countries. He would readily turn from discussing some archaeological problem to a new composition in music, or would discuss the latest trend in literature and the drama, or inquire as to the present turn of affairs in the world of labor. Every phase of life, and life in every corner of the globe, appealed to his eager mind. And yet the entire world of knowledge for him gathered under the Cross. This is a glorious privilege for the minister of any day, truly and sympathetically to be interested in world movements. This interest should rid him of petty personalities, of jealousies, which are too apt to creep into our noble vocation. Paul had the same keen and vigorous mind, interested in everything of the then known world, eager to see more of it, not content until the Cross was planted in the capital city of the world; he too is a picture of the pastor as man of the world. With Elizabeth Barrett Browning, the pastor finds meaning in the whole world:

"Earth's crammed with heaven,
And every common bush afire with God."

The pastor is to be the shepherd of his flock primarily, and yet he dare not let this group completely command him. He is to be interested in movements beyond the parish, so that they may lead him to wider horizons. As one of the two billion human beings on this planet the pastor ranks no higher than his congregation, but the obligation of a man who is attuned to Christ, Who came to draw all men unto Himself, is that his heart is to throb with the needs of men wherever they are. In this spirit he is to break down many of the barriers, parochial and denominational, which at present limit our endeavor.

Is the pastor to be a man of the world in the generally understood sense? A committee of laymen coming to ask for candidates to fill the pastorate of their church frequently gives as one of the qualifications that the pastor be a "good mixer." This is equivalent to the phrase at the head of this chapter. A man is desired for their pulpit who comes out of his study and lets himself be known as a man of human interests and appetites. He is to be a raconteur who always has a story fit for every occasion. In thinking back upon some of the men I have known in the ministry I recall them as being associated more with some neat story or witticism than with the expression of any great spiritual truth. The average man wants a pastor who is a good companion. If he makes eighteen holes of golf in ninety he will have the esteem of the entire club. When I entered into the student work at the universities an old friend of mine chided me for smoking before the young men. I spoke of it to the Rev. Dr. Cornelius Woelfkin, who as pastor of the Fifth Avenue Baptist Church and of the salt of the earth was one of my confidants. He said: "Fiddlesticks! The boys will like you better if you smoke." All the pursuits of the man of the world, in which the minister today is indulging more and more, bring about a very precarious condition in which each man must be his own arbiter. I have set forth the value of them, but I would also hold up the finger of admonition with reference to them.

The late Rev. Dr. Maltbie D. Babcock, pastor

of the Brick Church in New York, was one of the most spiritual men I have ever known; his sermons and his daily life expressed the eternal and the invisible.   In a sermon on the Christian and the world he used this illustration.   It is a beautiful sight, he said, to see a little child playing with her dolls; there is nothing wrong in it until the child becomes so absorbed by her toys that she no longer hears the voice of her mother.   It is then that her occupation with the dolls becomes harmful.   In the same way the pastor must be his own judge as to how far he may be lured into worldly pursuits.   When he no longer hears the still small voice calling him to the highest, then he is in danger of becoming engulfed.

There is still another phase of this matter that must be considered; it is the effect which certain indulgences have upon those of not particularly strong character.   St. Paul said that he would refrain from that which might cause his brother to stumble.   Influence is one of the most mysterious and far-reaching forces in our social life. There is not an adult who has not been startled on learning of the influence of some word or deed of whose influence he was unconscious, though it was great in the life of some bystander.   This is true of ministers to a heightened degree, and it should cause us to walk circumspectly even in most harmless occupations.

During the past months the *Churchman* has opened its columns to an age-long controversy which both amused and interested me. It comes up with an amazing regularity—the desirability of clothes of a distinctly clerical cut. This habit is always felt to set men aside as distinct ambassadors of Christ. It certainly does have that value if men conduct themselves in accordance with their calling, but what a shocking hiatus is produced when a man wearing this garb lacks the dignity of the minister, not to speak of the loveliness of Christ! Possibly it is a matter of temperament, changing even in the same individual during different periods of his life. In this connection I think of Phillips Brooks, who was America's greatest pastor and preacher. I love to think of him as wearing civilian clothes; these were a very minor matter with him. Through all his life and conversation, through the pictures of him, there remains the impression of a mighty man of God. Whether or not he wore a distinct garb, the consciousness of his great calling was so evident that no one could mistake him for merely a man of the world.

What the minister wears is purely an adiaphoron, and must be determined by the choice of the individual. No man should, however, depend upon his clothes to give validity to his calling. A soldier is happy in going into mufti, and it is a relief even for the man who habitually wears clerical garb sometimes to go into civilian clothing. Although I have always worn clericals on distinctly official occasions I have found it restful at other times to be simply one of the passing throng.

Our Lord was a "man of the world" in that it was said of Him, "Behold a man gluttonous, and a winebibber, a friend of publicans and sinners," which although untrue of Him showed that He was always where men needed Him. He was in the market place, at the receipt of custom, among the fishermen. He was wherever men were, but of Him it could be said, as it should be said of every true pastor, that He was there to seek and to save that which was lost. He was in the world but not of the world. This is a very precarious condition, but is made simple when Christ is in the heart of the pastor.

CHAPTER EIGHT

THE PASTOR AS CITIZEN

POLITICS is the rocky reef upon which many an eager young pastor wrecks his career. He takes his place in the community with the fresh enthusiasm of youth, but the response to his spiritual appeals rarely brings the results he expects. To a young man, impatient of result, such a drain on his patience is deadening. Around him are the many calls of the community that, besides filling every minute of the day with pursuits that appeal to his youthful spirit, give him the publicity which makes him known in that community as a conscientious public servant. In addition to this, every community endeavor awaits the new minister, and immediately gives him committee positions and chairmanships that threaten to break his back. Not only will these interests occupy him during the week, but gradually they will also creep into his preaching on Sunday. He must align himself with parties, and an expression from his pulpit will become partisan. So little by little he loses the satisfaction of bringing men that new sense of God which is his distinct vocation.

The kindly yet alert Philosopher of Beverly

Hills, who never left a hurt although his observations were keen, summed it up in these words:

"This is Monday, and I have been sitting here reading sermons delivered yesterday. On Sundays politics is transferred from the platform to the rostrum.

"In October, in election years, it's awful hard for a sinner, in search of spiritual advice, to drop into a church and receive any of it. Instead, he can hear an awful pretty theological talk on 'The NRA,' 'Fundamental Principles,' and 'Elect Brother Jones: He Will Lead Us Out of This Mire of Misery.'—Yours, Will Rogers."

Political preaching often entraps men in errors of statement that nullify all that they say. During a heated campaign in New York City on a Sunday night before election a minister waxed eloquent against William Travers Jerome, declaring he would never vote for Mr. Jerome. The candidate calmly remarked next day that the clerical brother in Brooklyn could never vote for him anyway, inasmuch as he was a candidate for the position only in Manhattan! The fact is no man can be a leader in every department of life. He must limit himself to certain spheres if he would be at all effective. Pastor caveat! Men who give themselves to covering the field of politics, from the community to world affairs, invariably and within a short period of time become very thin in what they have to say. They hold a group of people only for a short time. At the other extreme is the minister whose influence is completely that of the other world. He follows the Pauline injunction to have his conversation in heaven to such an extent that he does no more than whisper on earth. Not only is his life cloistered—everything he says has the same detachment. He belongs to a rapidly disappearing group of ministers who were invisible weekdays and incomprehensible Sundays. The number of such ministers is on the decline, whereas the group represented by the other extreme is very much on the incline. State Churches and their descendants in America stood for this conservative group; the free churches and their offspring were represented by the more liberal group.

Why should not the minister so deepen the content of his message that it would include both time and eternity? We have come to realize that eternal life is not so much a matter of time as of quality. The minister is to study God's will and then proclaim it. The will of God permeates the life of man. When the minister proclaims his message, he too often fails in following it through. He enunciates only the fundamental philosophy. If he should persist until it touched life at all points, the response would become more interesting and his message would have more regenerative value. The Christian has his duty to the State: he must be a conscientious voter; he must feel his social obligations toward the man living in the same apartment house with him as well as to the man on the other side of the world. On these great issues the minister must not hesitate. The religion he proclaims must be the working philosophy of his people for seven days of the week. His greatest trial comes when the dicta of Church and State conflict. The most trying example of this is taking place in the Germany of today, as is noted elsewhere.

During the World War the Church in every country fell down before her great task. Instead of preaching the gospel of love from their pulpits, preachers, almost without exception, helped their governments in engendering hate against their opponents. Churches and church halls were used as recruiting stations; church organizations sold Liberty Bonds. In every department the Church completely followed out the plans of the State. At such times the minister must show himself—even at the risk of his position and sometimes of his life—as one who serves the King of kings rather than any temporal ruler. In this most terrible of all catastrophes, when all of civilization is threatened to be swept away by war, the voice of the Christian Church must be heard above the demands of self-seeking politicians and munition-makers. That voice should always be on the side of the settlement of the world's differences by arbitration and other peaceful means. That one Christian nation should be immediately at the throat of another

Christian nation is a direct violation of the commandments of Christ.

In this connection I would commend to the consideration of all Church people the pledge that was taken by more than two hundred Protestant clergy and Jewish rabbis in the Riverside Church, New York City. This is the pledge:

"In loyalty to God I believe that the way of true religion cannot be reconciled with the way of war. In loyalty to my Country I support its adoption of the Kellogg-Briand Pact which renounces war. In the spirit of true patriotism and with deep personal conviction, I therefore renounce war, and never will I support another."

This pledge goes beyond my own position, but it represents leadership; it was born of careful and conscientious thought, and it brings the issue of war into the open so that men and women can make up their minds about a modern evil which, while it exists, remains an affront to the Christian Church and blasphemes the love of Christ.

The minister is first of all a Christian. There lies his obligation, and there must lie his allegiance. His citizenship is in Heaven. In his preaching and in his own personal life he must always have in view not the favor of certain individuals and groups but the welfare and happiness of every dweller on the globe. Said Terence:

"Homo sum; humani nihil a me alienum puto."
The minister, to whom nothing human is alien,
must use his deep feeling for humanity with intelligence. He must wisely weigh the rights of
every party; he must often risk the disfavor of his
congregation in his loyalty to some new or little-
heard-of movement. He will never rest content
with present achievement in world affairs, but
will of necessity belong to the group that presses
forward to secure righteousness and justice for
every man that is born in the image of God.

General William Booth once said that religion
has two purposes, one the comforting, the other
the inspirational. Men have turned to it when
other helpers failed and comforts fled, and they
have been sustained by it; but one wonders how
far men have been inspired by it. Possibly it
would seem here our ministers have been griev-
ously at fault. Are sermons definite, or do they
end in vain banalities, leaving the man in the pew
untouched by his duties as a Christian? The minister must make his people see their responsibility
to one another and to the State. He must whip
up their political conscience so that men will realize that their community is just exactly what
they make it.

The altar demands their presence, but so does
the ballot box or the voting machine. Some of
his flock will not see this last unless he says it
so plainly that they can make no mistake. The
Church must in clear terms defend her rights—

that is, Christian citizens must do so—otherwise the Church will have the fate that she is suffering in Russia, and which is threatening in Germany. The minister must be a citizen exercising his rights as well as enjoying the privileges of his country. He must inspire his people to do the same. It is then that we shall have a land in which the better element makes the laws.

In America, where Church and State are separated, we still have the anomaly of the Church being supported by the State to the extent of freedom from taxes. There is justification for this, and also there is much reason to put an end to it. Christian bodies are accused of abusing the privilege, and some surely are guilty of un-Christian practices in the face of the benevolence of the State. But, in any case, this largess on the part of the State demands that men of religion should give a specially generous return to the State in terms of a citizenry that is public-spirited and sacrificial. Do the members of a Christian congregation always measure up to this standard?

CHAPTER NINE

THE CHURCH AND YOUTH

THE Church is always dying—but she never dies. First-century Christians, certain of the end of the world, hastily snatched endangered souls from impending doom—but the world went on. Today Dr. Buchman and his Oxford Group—the modern First Century Christians—are preaching the joy of life in Christ, trying to change the world. The Church is always passing through dark ages, ages of superstition, ages of doubt— but her numbers increase. She is always corrupt —but she rises and puts on incorruption. She grows old and lifeless, but she regains her youth when her old men dream dreams and her young men see visions.

It is this life-and-death struggle within the Church that makes a survey of her activities so difficult. At one moment one rises on the wings of optimism; the next, one plunges into the pit of pessimism. Twenty-five million unchurched young people in the United States, two million without the normal right of working and the chance to build a career—here is cause for gloom. Thousands upon thousands of young people meeting in Church and college groups filled with

zeal to live the life of Christ in the world today—
here is cause for joy.

The Church of Jesus Christ is the Church of
Youth. Our Lord was only thirty-three when
He was crucified; the average age of His followers when He called them was twenty-five, accord-
ing to the estimate of one of our American
scholars, Dr. Burton Easton, New Testament
professor in the General Theological Seminary in
New York. The men who "turned the world up-
side down" in the Apostolic Age were young
men; today the men who are in revolt against the
wrongs of the world—economic chaos, social in-
justice, national and racial hatreds—are young
men. The new wine of youth is bursting the old
bottles of the Church, but if she quickly finds new
bottles she can catch this rich new life for the
service of Christ.

One is tempted to despair when one sees the
work of the Church done outside the Church and
by those who are against the Church. The Young
Communist International at its Sixth World
Congress in Moscow has called on the youth
of the world to unite against war. This youthful
organization, which claims to represent three
million six hundred thousand young Communists
throughout the world, has voiced an appeal that
every Christian knows he should not merely echo
but should proclaim even more loudly. Nineteen
hundred years after Christ died to unite the
world more than fifty-three million six hundred

thousand men are in the regular and reserve armies of the world, not counting the unknown millions more who are ready to spring to arms at the command of their governments. What could be more Christian than a call to end this traffic in death, even when the call is uttered by those who style themselves atheists? "He that is not against me is for me." Christ seeing young Communists helping to cast out the devil of war would again say, "Forbid them not," as He did when John said, "Master, we saw one casting out devils in thy name: and we forbade him, because he followed not us."

The shout of Communist youth may seem louder than that of Christian youth when we are in a pessimistic mood, but Christian youth has also been active against war—all war, not merely capitalist war, as is the Communist. In America we have had our peace parades and our pledges against war. All over the country young Church people are studying the causes of war and shaping their lives to the destruction of this menace to civilization. They are quite as earnest if not so audible as young Communists.

The Communist Party in Kiev, holding its quarterly examinations, had questions such as these:

"How many evenings a week do you give to the party?

"How many books have you read on Communism?

"How many technical books have you read?

"Have you ever converted anybody to Communism?"

Have we a Christian equivalent to such close questioning as this? Indeed we have. Those who are acquainted with the Churches and colleges of America know how young people meet in study groups to work out thoroughly their duties in the economic and social life of their day. They even sacrifice part of their vacations for this purpose by meeting in summer schools. One young New York clergyman who has spoken in forty colleges during the past eight years is struck by the increased interest of the students in economic and social questions, and by their spontaneous reaction to religion, as compared with the attitude of the students during his college days.

In this approach to the students the Lutheran Church has taken her share. In my own Synod, the United Lutheran Synod of New York, we have a chapel just by the entrance to the campus of Cornell University, built for the students. We have a pastor there devoting his full time to this work, and another in Boston ministering to the students attending Harvard University. At the conclusion of my first pastorate at the Church of the Messiah, Brooklyn, New York, I spent two years among the students of five great American universities—Harvard, Yale, Columbia, Cornell, and Syracuse. This work has developed, but its

full possibilities of growth are yet unrealized.
We have the men—more men are seeking ordination than the Church can call—but we lack the
money.

Sometimes we ask pessimistically, Where are
the leaders of the Church of Tomorrow? Possibly the pessimists of the Church in 325 A.D. were
asking the same question at the moment when
the young Athanasius, at the age of thirty-two,
was defending the Faith at the Council of Nicæa!
St. Francis of Assisi has emerged as one of the
Church's greatest evangelists; how many guessed
this when he founded his order at the age of
thirty-four? Did the Church realize when Luther
nailed his theses to the church door at Wittenberg that this young man would shake the world?
John and Charles Wesley were laughed at when
they went outside church walls to preach to the
people in the open air; just two overzealous young
men gone astray! William Booth as a young
man erecting a tent amid London's slums did not
look in the least like the first head of the world-
wide Salvation Army. Today when we look
around for our leaders we may find them among
the men and women we are criticizing or reject-
ing. It took the world a century to recognize
the greatness of Johann Sebastian Bach. If he
were not hailed as a world master of music in his
day, why should we claim any infallibility in the
recognition of the Church's leaders in the twentieth century?

When the Rich Young Ruler turned away sadly, unwilling to surrender his great possessions to follow Jesus, it might seem that the Church has some excuse for not winning the world for Christ, since there were occasions when even He failed to win disciples. The Church, however, must never use this excuse. Her Master said it was hard for a rich man to enter the kingdom of Heaven; He did not say it was impossible. Many New York society girls are much disturbed about their great possessions; some throw themselves into Church and social work, others join Communist classes. Christianity and Communism both inspire sacrifice; both seek to change the world; both are international.

The Spirit of God is eternally going forth to inspire the sons of men; youth, by reason of its idealism, sincerity, energy, responds. Yet here the present generation must keep the channels open for the entrance of the Spirit. The great ally of Luther in the Reformation was the printing press. He kept that new invention working overtime. We have not yet caught up to him—not to speak of motion pictures and the radio. Dean Ackerman of the Columbia University School of Journalism recently told me that the Protestant Church is making but a superficial experiment in developing the untold possibilities of the radio as a means of spreading truth. Better investment the Church cannot make than to have a corps of able scholars constantly interpreting the eternal truth into the changing language of the coming generation. Our faith is to provide wings, not to be a weight. Another corps of writers should portray in attractive biographies the life of present-day saints. Youth asks, "Is it possible to live a life in Christ in the twentieth century?" Such a life as that of Albert Schweitzer answers, "Yes!" Let more such lives be written to spur on our young people to emulate the Church's saints and heroes! What a story the Rev. Dr. John A. Morehead, who welded the Lutheran Churches of the world together in the Lutheran World Convention, could write—and, I believe, will write! What a romantic tale he could tell out of his unique and rich experiences of ministering to the churches in war-stricken Europe, and in many subsequent visits during the reconstruction period.

We must elevate our worship, be it ritualistic or simple. The Eucharistic Congress in Cleveland, Ohio, held in the fall of 1935, gave a fine example of this. The worshiper coming in faith, expectant, receives the blessing. Pastor and people too often let the hours of worship pass by in deadly mediocrity. The entire conception must be lifted. Men must feel themselves on holy ground, in the presence of the Eternal, in their worship. Sermons must be designed with that definite purpose. We tremble as we realize how much the life of the coming generation hangs on the pastors of the present generation. Woe to that Church whose watchmen in the towers have fallen asleep!

So that the Spirit of God may dwell therein, the Church must be honest beyond earthly standards. She must not hide behind prejudice; she must unflinchingly speak her convictions; she must resist unrelentingly political-minded groups in her midst who seek to impose their selfish ends. Nothing alienates idealistic youth so much as lack of sincerity in the Church. A leader of one denomination said recently, "Men do not love the Church, because she is not lovely." The Church must be kept "without spot or wrinkle or any such thing."

The coming generation must be represented more strongly in the councils of the Church. We need the balance and wisdom that older men give, but we need also the energy and the vision of younger men. The Church is too much in the care of older men. The sway of youth in the chancelleries of Europe is remarkable. Schuschnigg, Chancellor of Austria, is thirty-eight years old; Van Zeeland, of Belgium, and Salazar, of Portugal, are both forty-two; while Hitler, of Germany, is only forty-six. Gil Robles, of Spain, is thirty-six; and Anthony Eden, of England, is thirty-eight. Compared with these Mussolini, at fifty-two, is one of the elder statesmen, topped by Stalin at the age of fifty-six. The Church becomes too conservative with only the older statesmen at the helm. She is prone to lose the sympathy of the coming generation.

It is the imperative duty of the Church to show young people that the Master's "Go ye into all the world!" is greater than Karl Marx's "Workers of the world, unite!" She must show that the power of Jesus to win the world is greater than that of Lenin and Stalin. She must win by a wider vision and a more loving endurance. And everywhere she must believe that the Kingdom of God is ready to break in upon the world; that men can bring a new spirit into the work of the world and into their relations with the nations and races of the world. This is work for youth, because youth has faith enough to change the world.

CHAPTER TEN

NEW PROBLEMS OF CHURCH AND STATE

THE Church has a new problem that threatens her very life. This is the problem of the totalitarian State. In the face of this new political challenge one wonders whether the Church will live or die in these increasing totalitarian States. I determined in the late fall of 1934 to investigate for myself the life of the Church in two of these countries. I flew from Berlin to Moscow on November 6, the last flight of the season, in order to be present at the celebration of the seventeenth anniversary of the Revolution on the following day. My first touch with Russia, however, was unexpected and precipitous. By reason of the increasing storm and the blackening darkness, together with a radio message from Moscow, our two pilots, German and Russian, risked a landing early in the afternoon at an airport under construction at Welikiye Luki, where there was no provision for passengers. Although I was disappointed in not reaching Moscow that night, later I felt repaid for having had this experience at this Russian outpost. The surrounding district was barren, and we had food only because some German engineers, who had come to mend a broken plane, shared the contents of their knap-sacks with us. As we found our way through the mud and the darkness to a peasant house three hundred yards away, where we were to find shelter, we passed a Russian sentry with gun over his shoulder pacing in front of the small village commissary. This made me feel the preciousness of food in rural Soviet Russia.

The next morning, at daybreak, the pilots decided to attempt to continue the flight despite the fact that the weather was still far from favorable. We were suffering from the stress and strain of our nerve-racking experience of the previous day, and a troubled night, and feeling far from secure in this giant plane, of which we were now the sole passengers, entirely cut off from the two pilots. Dr. Devol, who was seated on the other side of the plane from me, suddenly leaned over, placed his hand on my shoulder, and said, with perfect sincerity, "If we ever land at Moscow alive I will devote the remainder of my life to righteous living and good deeds." Soon after, the clouds began to lift and we were flying smoothly over the forests and plains and rivers of Russia, which so enchanted us that before we realized it we were over the city of Moscow. We were a bit perplexed to know why the pilots flew round and round unless it was to show us the multiple streams of marching humanity converging toward the Red Square, where Stalin at that very moment was reviewing the troops. We later learned that the real reason of this postponement of our landing was due to an order that our pilots had received to display the plane, one of the prize planes of Russia, to the great multitudes of people.

On landing we were courteously received by an Intourist guide who spoke English perfectly. He had lived part of his life in Bridgeport, Connecticut. We were rushed through customs, our baggage thoroughly mauled over by a woman inspector. In a Lincoln car we were piloted through throngs of people to our hotel. By this time the irritation produced by so much red tape had, alas, made the pious resolve of my friend Dr. Devol vanish—as is so apt to happen in life when resolves are made under such stress!

Throughout that day we watched the parade of the Russian Army and Navy, together with the airplanes, before Stalin standing at the tomb of Lenin in the Red Square. It was a parade which made the maneuvers of the German Army before Emperor William II, which I had seen in 1908, seem outmoded and outnumbered. The second day was given to the parade of the civic organizations, all of which begat an almost delirious joy, especially on the part of the young people. There was the new, all-powerful State bringing new opportunities to the working class of Russia. It was only on the next day that I could make my way through the crowds to see one of our Lutheran churches with its pastor. What a con-

trast! It was one of the few churches still remaining after the various processes of "liquida-
tion." The building itself had been one of the
stately structures of the Czarist régime but was
now so dilapidated that it typified the condition
of religion throughout the Soviet Union. The
pastor was so fearful of the future that he would
rather not have spoken. He charged me, moreover, not to divulge his name either in Russia or
in America. Our interpreter, a young Russian
Communist, said to have belonged to the old
aristocracy, kept so close to us that it was with
difficulty that the pastor was able to whisper in
German to me, "Come to the church tomorrow,
without the interpreter." When I made that visit,
he told me of the experiences of the Church in
Russia, which were "only to be described by the
language of the Book of the Apocalypse."

On the way out to see him I visited the grave
of Bishop Meyer, who died in the spring of 1934
after having given himself gallantly to the main-
tenance of the life of the Church in Russia.
Lenin, the founder of the Soviet State, had declared the Church to be an instrument of the
wealthy classes for the oppression of the working
class, and that all churches must go. One could
feel the clamps being applied, paralleling the
days of the Inquisition, the Church gradually
expiring under this fearful pressure. Walter
Duranty told me at the time that the Soviet
régime was the most remarkable economic ex-

periment of the ages. Certainly much of what is being done for the people is commendable. At the same time, the Soviet State is a brutal organization. In its program the Church of the gentle Nazarene has no place. Here is a real challenge to the Church of today—shall 168,000,000 Russians grow into an entirely Godless life? Will the embalmed body of Lenin, which attracts an endless line of worshipers, suffice to give this great nation the inspiration and hope which every soul needs?

The pastor of the Lutheran Church of St. Peter, on the Nevski Prospect in Leningrad, graciously gathered for me the six remaining Lutheran pastors of that district, when I visited him, and together they presented a more hopeful picture for religion. The church building itself still retained its beauty, including its famous Holbein altarpiece. At the Third Lutheran World Convention in Paris, October, 1935, the report was made that only eight Lutheran pastors were still functioning in Russia. I wondered whether some of these valiant young messengers of the Cross were still at their posts. The theological seminary which had provided ministers for these stricken congregations under the leadership of Bishop Malmgren, that noble soul, had even then been abandoned, and this prospect had reached a dead end.

I turned westward from Russia, wearied with the propaganda and the restlessness of this new

venture, and was glad to be again in some of the
countries where more conservative methods pre-
vailed. In Riga, which had successfully repulsed
the Revolution, I called on Bishop Poelschau; at
Danzig I talked for some time with Bishop Beer-
mann; at Königsberg I stood at the tomb of Kant.
I finally found myself again in Berlin. But here,
too, I had to deal with the restlessness that comes
with a new venture. It was extremely interesting, and Berlin during those days made any other
world capital seem very tame. On my first day I
drank coffee in the same dining-room with Hitler.
As the only strangers among the few people present, he carefully studied my friend Dr. Devol and
myself, and we in turn had a close-range scrutiny
of Der Führer.

In Germany, as in Russia, one saw the center-
ing of political power in one man or a small group
of men, and everything had either been coördinated with this plan or been "liquidated." We
came to know many of the leading political fig-
ures, such as Propaganda Minister Göbbels, Foreign Minister von Neurath, Alfred Rosenberg,
leader of the Neo-Pagan movement, Ernst Hanf-
stängel, head of the foreign press, as well as our
own ambassador, Mr. William E. Dodd, a scholar
and diplomat, and the English ambassador, Sir
Eric Phipps. Just before sailing from America I
had been notified by the Oberländer Foundation,
created by Mr. Gustav Oberländer for the purpose of fostering friendly relations between the

two countries, that I had been made a fellow of this worthy philanthropy. This hospitable organization proved a great help to me. Many introductions to men in both Church and State were made possible by this foundation. Nothing was left undone to make me comfortable while in Germany.

It was interesting to see a nation being coördinated with so little open friction. The Church, however, stood out against this coördinating influence. With the patience that is characteristic of the German, the churchmen of Germany had first tried to run with the hare and hunt with the hounds, but when it dawned upon them that this movement would mean the emasculation of their faith, they quietly but firmly resolved to take their stand. It is said that when two pastors in Germany meet at the present time their friendship is confirmed if they have both had prison experience. The State started by attempting to reach its goal through a Nazi Church, the German Christian Church, but this has weakened almost to disappearance. Again, the State hoped to put off the day of decision by appointing a committee of adjustment. In the meantime the Church is being stirred, and no matter what the end may be, the Christians of Germany have come to a new valuation of their faith.

During the month I was in Berlin I went each Sunday to Dahlem to hear the Rev. Martin Niemöller, former U-boat Captain, and the sturdy champion of the Confessional Church. With men of his spirit one has no occasion to fear for the future of Christianity in Germany, and I met many such throughout the Reich.

I went to Dresden to visit Baron von Kirchbach, who had been court preacher, but had been deposed, and now was holding services of worship in a hall. From there to Leipzig, where I consulted with the theological faculty at the university, then on to Hanover to visit with Bishop Marahrens, and the following day to Bielefeld, where I spent the night in this greatest "Colony of Mercy." I had known Pastor Bodelschwing in former years, but was impressed anew by his consecrated leadership. I came away understanding why he preferred this priceless legacy from his father to being the Reichsbishop of Germany.

The outcome of the struggle in Germany may be the separation of Church and State, which to the outsider would seem desirable; but one cannot feel that the German nation will dispense with the Gospel which one of her greatest sons, Martin Luther, restored to the world.

I crossed the Rhine on my way home feeling in my heart an increasing affection and admiration for the great German people, their patience and willingness to suffer for an ideal. The most vivid picture that remains with me from my sojourn in Germany is the noble army of martyrs and heroes of the faith who are rising up in every part of the Reich. They are men of apostolic mold, and the result of their life and prayer may bring a new Reformation. They are unafraid and face hunger and imprisonment as glorious opportunities to witness for their faith.

Some of them were leaders in the World War —men of disciplined mind and quiet action. They are not taking their stand for sensational effect. They guard carefully against any political disgruntlement expressing itself through the Church. They prefer to make no public statements, and they wait patiently the leading of God, in Whose word alone they trust. One's mind goes back four hundred years to the Wittenberg monk who stood before Charles V at Worms and declared: "Here I stand. I cannot do otherwise. God help me."

CHAPTER ELEVEN

THE USE AND ABUSE OF MONEY

Skillful navigation is required to keep clear of the Scylla of affluence and the Charybdis of poverty. I have seen more ministers shipwrecked in financial waters than in any other of the strange and difficult seas and storms they encounter in the course of their vocation. Whether they are wrecked by affluence or by poverty, they are in either case destroyed by their wrong ideas about money.

Picture the minister who has built up his church, winning an ever widening hearing for his message. Perhaps he is tempted by his success to go into some easy speculation whereby he may educate his children or put by a comfortable sum for his old age. The stock market is strong, and he feels himself remiss in not having entered this "harmless" activity before. Furthermore, he may take money from his flock, who trust him implicitly to invest it for them. He gradually begins to frequent the brokerage offices until some day, even with the best of counsel, he finds himself with a wrong investment, or the entire market breaks as it did in 1929. He feels grotesquely like a fleeced lamb in an uncommonly bitter winter's wind! He begins to borrow money to cover his deal, and so increasingly alienates some of his best friends. Because of their innocence of the methods of Wall Street, ministers suffer more severely when they are caught in its cruel claws. My father gave me the cherished counsel that a Christian pastor should never enter into any business venture. He told me, "You should find all your energies occupied by your vocation as a minister." I should like to pass on that injunction to the ministers of the present day.

Paul writes his spiritual son, Timothy, "The love of money is the root of all evil." On the other hand, the minister dare not ignore the fact of money and its relation to him. It intrudes itself and must be recognized. There are countless men, for the most part of simple faith, who go under in their ministry because they do not count the cost before they build the tower. Some men emerge from their training with a heavy load of debt resting on their shoulders, a debt they have bravely assumed so as to complete their education. Without freeing themselves of this debt they immediately plunge into marriage and involve themselves in an establishment which is beyond their means. They are compelled to borrow money, which they find it more and more impossible to repay. The community soon becomes conscious of the minister's plight, and he is apt to lose his standing. The Apostle Paul counsels his followers, "Owe no man anything but to love one another." That should be the special duty of the spiritual leader.

Then there is the minister who is so shrewd in his financial affairs, or the fates have heaped upon him such wealth, that in his early middle life, when he should be making his richest contribution to the Church, he finds himself with some imaginary sickness, and he retires to spend the rest of his life in luxury and lack of purpose. Introspectively he spends all of his energy in nursing his own complaints, and from that time on he cumbers the ground. Had he not been "cursed" with so much money his life would have continued happily in the pursuit of his great vocation.

The pastor of the flock, however, must also be the guide of his people when it comes to the expenditure of money on the part of the congregation. Just before the present depression the Church had entered upon a debauch of new building which equaled the institutions of the world about her. Today one can still hear the cracking of bones as the cruel conditions of the time are squeezing pastors and congregations for the sin of overbuilding into which they went during those wild years after the World War. Churches are always apt to overbuild instead of putting the like effort into paying adequate salaries to their staff. The same evil is seen in institutions of learning when the campus is cluttered with new

buildings instead of funds being put aside to secure the very best teachers. One often wonders
whether this depression has taught people much
as to the art of living. So one wonders whether
congregations have learned anything as to the
relative value of their efforts.

This almost unlicensed building has brought
upon the Church the plague of unchurchly practices in raising money to meet these almost insuperable burdens. One's heart goes out to the
faithful people who are willing to do anything to
turn a penny that shall reduce the interest or
principal on these ventures, but one's heart goes
out still more to them when one realizes that at
the end of all their effort they have done little
that will help along the spiritual purpose of the
Church, and that they may have done more evil
than they have accomplished good. I am thinking of bazaars, card parties, dances, lotteries, for
the sake of raising money, many of which are a
stench in the nostrils of the world, and which
often so exhaust the people who take part in them
that they have no strength reserved for the great
purposes of the Christian life.

There is still one impact of money upon the
minister's life which may be his undoing. It is
the man or the woman in the congregation who
pays the largest sum to the support of the work,
and who also would thereby dictate the entire
policy of the congregation. I was happily as free
of this in my church that included men of large

wealth as I was in my parish where every man was a wage-earner. Not every man, however, has this happy fortune; to overcome it requires God-given tact. The pastor must remain the spiritual leader of the congregation; his ideals must be those that determine what the church is to be. When a pastor is confronted by one who would dominate the church's policy he does well to pray over the matter fervently, and then discuss it frankly with the person in question. He can introduce all the sympathetic understanding of which he is capable, but withal he must be firm. He is acting not for himself but for his Lord, Who said many hard things about money —hard from the point of view of those who worship money—and Who always placed spiritual values on heights to which money alone could never reach. And it is toward the triumph of the spiritual that the pastor must bend every effort, leading his congregation to their Master.

CHAPTER TWELVE

THE CHURCH AND PUBLICITY

WHEN Jesus told His disciples to go throughout the world preaching the good news, He settled the question of publicity once and for all time. The Church has a message to proclaim and she must seize every available means of telling it to the world. She must not adopt a shy and shrinking attitude. That which she would have proclaimed from the housetops of our Lord's day she must send forth from skyscraper radio stations in the twentieth century. The whole planet must hear the message of Christ.

The conception of publicity as we understand it today is quite young. And with it has come such a deluge of words, of printed matter, of radio periods, that the average man no longer thinks, or has the time to think. Everything is dumped into his mind ready for consumption. The most striking instance of this takes place in governments such as Germany and Russia where free thought is severely censored, and where every impression upon the citizen is that which has been prepared by those above. It is a far cry from the grocery store at the crossroads, where on a winter evening a man freely discussed the affairs of the community, to the present day, when the slightest whisper is detected and controlled.

The Church too has adopted this modern method of making herself known. The press and the radio have shown friendliness to the Church, and have lent themselves in generous fashion to her purpose. Some of this propaganda is helpful, and some of it harms; most of it is very superficial. It is always in danger of usurping the real witness to Christianity, which must lie in the lives of those who bear the name of Christ. It is even in danger of displacing the object of our faith, Christ Himself, by the question as to how many columns in the papers, and how many periods on the radio, can be secured. This shows to what an absurd length the entire problem of publicity may run if it is dealt with only as an object in itself. Christ's method of propaganda remains the one to follow; it is the fundamental one of preaching the good tidings. Nothing can supersede the voice of man for propagating the message and building up the Kingdom of God. This can always be a comfort to such as feel the call of God to preach His message. The world has to be converted by men who are possessed by the thought of God. The more that truth controls the preacher, the more effective will be his ministration. With a man so fired with his message the effect must be contagious. Peter's sermon on the Day of Pentecost brought three thou-

sand converts; fervid preaching has always succeeded in bringing men into the Church.

The next step in publicity will come through
the lives of the disciples. This is often a more
effective method than that of preaching. The
world judges the Christian way of life by the life
of the Christian. "Let your light so shine before
men that they may see your good works, and
glorify your Father which is in heaven." Here
also Jesus emphasized that no attempt must be
made to cover up the lives of true Christians,
which must be so glorious that the truths of a
religion which produces such results will be
spread far and wide. "Ye are the light of the
world. A city set on a hill cannot be hid. Neither
do men light a lamp and put it under a bushel,
but on a stand; and it shineth unto all that are in
the house."

All this will be admitted. It is fundamental.
Without genuine Christian lives the most perfect
system of propaganda and publicity that the most
brilliant brains in the Church can devise will be
worse than useless. Christianity is far more than
right ideas about God and man; it is the expression of those ideas in the changed lives of men.

We cannot end, however, with the admission
of this fact. Men are changed not only by hearing the good news and by example but also by
taking part in the worship of God. Contact is
established not only by man to man but also by
the services of the Church. It is possible to con-

ceive of a service in a Christian church being so beautiful—the music so full of worship, the sermon so sincere—that a man with evil in his heart would be powerless to go forth and execute the ugly deed that he had planned. It is possible, even in the midst of war and the fierce passions then aroused, that the Christian Church could by her services proclaim the presence of a God greater than the tribal gods now worshiped by the nations, could draw men to the worship of the Father of Jesus Christ, the God Who is the Father of all men and nations.

Besides the lives of her saints and of her members, the Church could reveal God to the world by her devotional services. In music alone the Church has a message that could save the world. The Church does not begin to use the rich treasures of her music—even in those churches where the musical side of worship is by no means neglected. Music, like the life of a Christian, can be a "light" reaching into the dark corners of the world. Not music used merely to draw big congregations but music so good and true and beautiful in itself that it will act upon men in the same way that the true Christian acts upon them. Day after day, throughout the year, not Sundays only, such music could proclaim the glory and the wonder of God.

After having thoroughly established the sincere preaching of the Word, the witness that every Christian must bear to the truth which she professes, and the Church's devout worship— after having established these three fundamentals, then the Church is justified in utilizing every method which she can find to proclaim the Gospel of Jesus Christ; by sermons and street preaching; by stage plays, movies, radio; by letters, leaflets, newspapers, magazines, pamphlets, books. Books of the highest literary merit, yet popular enough to be listed among the best-sellers, should be written to reach a wide public.

The tremendous new opportunity afforded by newspaper and radio has extended the range of the preacher's message from his visible congregation to his invisible audience. The Rev. Dr. S. Parkes Cadman, brilliant leader and radio preacher, stated that during one radio sermon he reached as many people as his father had reached in the forty years of his ministry in Great Britain. The Rev. Dr. Henry Howard, one of a line of outstanding preachers at the Fifth Avenue Presbyterian Church, New York, said to Miss Rachel K. McDowell, religious editor of the New York *Times*, "You have given wings to my erstwhile pedestrian words." How can any zealous disciple of the twentieth century, aflame with his message, resist the opportunity of using such methods for the multiplying of his influence? General Church bodies must have definite policies to utilize these powerful instruments. Publicity should center in the message and not in the

person. With such tremendous possibilities before her for the spreading of her truth the Church
would do well to have a full-time staff to interpret
her message for the eyes and ears of those who
would receive it by press and radio. We ordain
pastors to take care of a flock of two to three
hundred people; why should we not have men
ordained to care for the larger invisible parish?
The Roman Catholic Church requires at least
one seminary student in every diocese to attend a
school of journalism during the summer, if not
longer. Thus does the Church, by studying publicity methods, adapt herself to these new opportunities.

Benjamin Harris, who published the first
American newspaper in 1690, recognized that
Church and Press had a common task, the main-
tenance and extension of moral and spiritual
standards. In *Publick Occurrances* he promised to
relate faithfully the memorable occurrences of a
Divine Providence in order that "people everywhere may better understand the circumstances
of Publique Affairs both abroad and at home."
He said also that he wanted to do something toward "the Curing or at least the Charming of
that Spirit of Lying which prevails amongst us."

It is indeed true that the Church has the task
of maintaining and extending moral and spiritual
standards. In this she can enlist the aid of press
and radio, not so much by the criticism of either,
or both, as by making her own contributions to

newspaper columns and radio periods beyond reproach. Churchmen involved in scandals, sects squabbling about their differences instead of uniting on their common beliefs, get plenty of publicity—front-page stuff, some of it—but it were better for the Church to be hidden in the catacombs, serving her Master, than that she should achieve only that kind of publicity.

"Stop thinking in terms of publicity, headlines, and space, and think in terms of ideas," said Dean Carl Ackerman, of the School of Journalism at Columbia University. "A newspaper story or a radio hour which is not an integral part of a carefully planned program with a definite objective of public education or edification related directly to the lives of the people; news stories or radio talks designed chiefly to fill space, attract attention, or consume time for so-called advertising purposes, are not worth time or effort. Continuity of interest and unity of news are becoming more important. The Church needs a long-term editorial policy, not a fly-by-night, catch-as-catch-can publicity policy."

The pastor will naturally establish newspaper and radio contacts, but he will understand that anything he does or says will be printed or broadcast only in so far as it is news—something new, new action, new ideas, new facts, new activities, something of public interest. He may have to wait for recognition, but this will certainly come if he does something worth while, or says something worth while.   If he refuses to compromise he will eventually win the respect of men, and will draw them upward.

The Church can afford to wait. Her message is not of today or tomorrow but of eternity.

CHAPTER THIRTEEN

THE PROBLEM OF LEISURE

THE world has never before known the amount of leisure it has at present. One who goes back several generations finds every soul in the community seriously occupied with the making of a living. There was very little time to unbend; the average person knew nothing of leisure. A living was to be won only by the most stubborn fighting with conditions; any letup in this struggle would mean the undoing of the individual. There was a niche for every worker. Trained men took their places, untrained men fell naturally into their grooves. Children from the first period of responsibility were asked to make their contribution. Each child was an asset and quickly returned the small amount expended on it. In this way every community presented a picture of a solid front of labor. Even the professions of preaching and teaching were not exempt from physical work. Pastors were compelled to supplement their small incomes by farming. This condition lasted until our communities began to be industrialized. Men could not keep machines running all the time, because of nervous exhaustion. The machinery had to

be repaired, also, and so the almost endless work
hours of the previous era began to be limited.
Men worked fourteen hours a day, then eight
hours; now the demand is for a thirty-hour week.
This means that only a fifth of the time of the
average toiler will be occupied in his work. It is
but a third of the time his father gave to his
occupation.

But here we have not considered the large
number of workers who during the depression
have been fitfully occupied or not occupied at all.
In our own land this means one-tenth of the
population or one-third of the people who are
normally at work; furthermore, for some time
there will be sundry millions of the unemployed.

This complicated pattern of life today gives
some idea of the amount of free time that the
world has at its disposal. What is to be done
with it? Shall we allow men to become flabby,
physically as well as spiritually, in the face of
nothing to do? Shall they spend each day at
some cheap movie or sitting on park benches?
Warden Lawes, of Sing Sing, has pointed out
that it is not so much the education of young people that we must watch, it is their recreation.
The question of the people's recreation should
concern the Christian man or woman especially,
as one who loves men and would serve them. Our
municipalities have been making experiments
with the problem. They have organized
orchestral concerts in various centers; they have

arranged for more recreation and games in our parks. They have organized artistic pursuits, which the skeptical call boondoggling. All these devices are commendable; they have not only cultivated in the individual some new love of beauty but they are factors in keeping the idle man out of mischief. It speaks rather well for human kind that during this recent depression, and consequent unemployment, there has not been more breaking of the law. With no responsibility resting upon so many of our citizens, it is quite easy to think of them as entering nefarious occupations; but to the credit of their character the great majority of them have been buoyed up by the hope of again obtaining regular employment, and they have refrained from making themselves socially undesirable.

Here lies a new responsibility and a rich opportunity for the Church. The minister must persistently and intelligently put before his people the diverse appeal of human needs. These can now be met so much more satisfactorily since not every minute of a man's life must be spent with his nose to the grindstone of making a living. He now has opportunity for cultivating qualities that had been almost completely atrophied. The love of the arts is to be revitalized by the radio, which now touches the remotest settlement. Everyone can enjoy the symphonies of Beethoven. A whole winter season can be enriched by following some symphony orchestra.

Here is but one of the many doors thrown open to the new generation, which has so much to bless it.

And yet the same opportunities, otherwise used, might easily work mischief. Hence the Church, above all other institutions, should be alert to make use of the opportunities afforded by this new era. In days gone by the weary workman was so fatigued at the end of his week that he was scarcely open to spiritual stimuli. The man of the modern age of leisure may come to his worship not any more fitted than the man of generations ago; but the Church can, if she makes her worship distinctive, her message impressive, win him back to her. By reason of the fact that nowhere else can he get the inspiration to be derived from worship he may return to the Church. If we let our services go to seed they will certainly count for nothing in the strenuous competition that the world is putting forth to employ the new leisure which has fallen upon the race. One need but look at the new moving-picture palaces that are being erected, and to the radio offerings constantly being made, to see that the Church, unless she lives up to her opportunity, will certainly fail to hold on. She may hold the traditional group, but young people who are reshaping their lives will not consider her appeal.

What an added strength the Church of the coming generation will have if she is alert enough to put forth her supreme claim upon the time and the life of man! The old excuse, with which practically everyone fortified himself, was that of having no time to do the things he wanted to do. In the presence of the considerable leisure available today this excuse no longer holds. The tenure of life seems to be lengthening now that less of it is given to the earning of daily bread. In former days the work of the Church was left largely to women because they alone had leisure time. Today the masculine element should show itself in the life of the Church. Church work should become a reality, not merely a phantom of other occupations. All this, however, depends upon the vitality and the intelligence with which the Church puts forth her claim. With this more abundant time at the disposal of the average citizen the Church should get out of her normal routine of having but one day of the week organized. There should be weekday services, there should be classes for the study of the Church functions; the church building itself should be an everyday invitation to men and women. This may seem Utopian, but it can be worked through if the Church once takes her business seriously, and realizes her position as the supreme one in our present society.

CHAPTER FOURTEEN

THE RECREATIONS OF THE MINISTER

LIFE has become tragic for a minister when he is compelled to seek pastime. For a man whose life is to be so crowded with things past, present, and future, with the affairs of his inner life and his outer life, there should be no occasion to kill time. Rather should his experience be that described by Robert Louis Stevenson:

"The world is so full of a number of things,
I'm sure we should all be as happy as kings."

The days and the years are never sufficient to care for all the interests of a minister.

The minister, however, should have some periods of recreation during which he can gain fresh life for body and mind, renewing his enthusiasm for the opportunities of life. It is by changing one's interests that this is accomplished, and the minister must systematically have such recreations at hand to prevent his becoming entirely exhausted with his work, and losing his zest for it.

Mrs. James Roosevelt tells of finding the future President of the United States, then nine years old, lying on the floor with the dictionary in front of him. When she asked what he was doing Franklin replied, "I am reading the dictionary, but I am only halfway through." No wonder that this recreation has resulted in the perfect diction that the President now uses! This study and wrestling with words is a sport that never loses its zest. Words have chapters of history behind them, the tragedies and achievements of the race, its failures and fresh beginnings. The study of the dictionary, together with Roget's Thesaurus and other more modern studies of words, is a compensating recreation, and makes the minister prize anew those wonderful tools which await the spread of his ideas.

Then, of course, the richest recreation in which anyone can sharpen his wits and again find the joy of his work is in books. The love of books is an essential qualification for the success of a minister. They are essential for his study and for his recreation. It is distressing to find some ministers' libraries consisting mostly of well-thumbed popular commentaries and a few books of sermons. The larger cultural collection that should reflect the life of the minister is absent. His habits are reflected when instead of seeking recreation through the companionship of the world's great men he consorts with the men at the corner cigar store or the village garage. What an enriching experience it is in adult life again to follow the classics one studied at college, where, at that time, they were a fearful chore, read for syntax and technical construction. What a privilege it is now to go over them, either in translation or in the original, to enjoy the satisfaction of the argument. The poor German schoolmaster who lived in a humble house in a small village could have over his doorway this proud inscription, "Dante, Molière, and Goethe live here." That schoolmaster had learned of the riches open to the poorest man.

Biography has been my preferred reading. What a world of new motives, both good and bad, are thrust before us in the numerous biographies that are before the reader these days! Each of them is a new experience that opens up vistas, not only of the world but of man's soul, in an alluring fashion. I always have a new regard for a minister if on entering his study I see somewhere a volume not connected with his next Sunday's sermon lying at hand, showing evidence of its being read at that time. It shows that the minister is preparing himself for his work and not simply preparing next Sunday's sermon.

The poet should be the preacher's most intimate associate. Great preachers have always had the poetic in them, and the best poets have been great preachers. It should be a refreshing recreation, as one's thought becomes stale, to lose oneself in the great poets—Dante, Shakespeare, Milton, Goethe, Browning, Walt Whitman, Kipling, Emily Dickinson, Francis Thompson, John Masefield, Edna St. Vincent Millay, Mary Cummings Eudy. Half an hour with any one of these poets clarifies the mind and gives it new instruments for good thinking. At our beckoning any one of these will come to refresh us.

Happy is the minister who can at times completely isolate himself from his work by travel! Even a simple excursion may yield great benefit and inspiration. In Europe one sees more people content to hike than one finds here. What refreshment and stimulation many extract from this recreation! One never fails to see them entering some village with their guidebooks, immediately mastering the scene. Its history, its quaint buildings, immediately open up to them. And what healthy appetites they bring with them! How many a "roadmender" they find whose philosophy is so fundamental that it cannot be gainsaid! Each day is a new chapter in their lives. There are still many unexplored parts of America that would richly compensate any hiking excursion, and if one goes abroad any country will generously repay such an effort.

Only second to such an expedition is the motor holiday, which is more and more becoming an outlet for every American. It is surprising to see how well our country is covered with splendid motor roads, which, however, plus the new cars, bring with them the danger of proceeding too rapidly over interesting territory. Men can drive

across the continent in a week, but they reach
their destination with very little knowledge of
the intervening country, and with a speed almost
devastating. The danger of our age is this head-
long speed, resulting, as it does, in our getting so
little out of travel; and I would warn the many
pastors who are able to take such a holiday each
year. Are they getting the joy and inspiration,
the new enthusiasm, to be found all along the
way, if they travel under such exacting conditions?

Oversea travel heightens the enjoyment and
satisfaction of leisure. I began it quite early in
my ministry, and it has always been my highest
anticipation and richest satisfaction. It offers
opportunities for friendships; among the people
I have met on my travels are some of my oldest
friends. It offers acquaintance with the colorful
conditions of other countries. It brings the les-
son that in every land, even in lands maligned,
there are men and women of simple charm, of
utmost courtesy, and of honest purpose, people
who seek the welfare of the race quite as much
as do those who speak our own language and
who live in houses like our own. In the years
since the World War the interest in the colorful
has gone out of European travel, to a certain extent. Every land is at present battling with its
seemingly insuperable problems. Visiting these
countries in their present disturbed condition,
one's sympathies are aroused, and one's convic-

tion reëstablished that God "hath made of one blood all nations of men for to dwell on all the face of the earth." The abiding value of travel is the growth of an understanding of every race, irrespective of creed, color, or historical background; it is of especial value to the American minister whose whole life is spent in contact with the sons of these countries. I came to have an entirely new regard for the men with whom I worked both as pastor in my two parishes and as executive in the Church after I learned the history of the lands from which they came. Such travel takes one out of the orbit of one's daily routine, and gives one a fresh vision of movements in the world. One cannot return to the normal routine without a new grasp and a more intimate understanding of men.

It is also a salutary excursion for the minister from time to time to step out of the circle in which he is the controlling influence and enter into circles where he is but one of a number of men. This is the value of friends. The minister must at times absolutely forget himself by entering into their experiences. By so doing he will put at naught the narrowness that is only too characteristic of ministers. Spending an evening in a circle such as this will widen the minister's horizon and make him sympathetic with the points of view of other men. Most ministers spend all their days in contact only with those who think as they do, and in this way they become narrow and dogmatic.

Of the refining and refreshing influence of the arts not enough can be said. The study of music should come at some time in the preparation of the minister, and happy is the man who understands music well enough to express himself through the voice or some instrument. While this is limited to a small group yet every man should have an appreciation of this noble art.

"The man that hath no music in himself,
  Nor is not moved by concord of sweet sounds,
  Is fit for treasons, stratagems, and spoils;
  The motions of his spirit are dull as night,
  And his affections dark as Erebus.
  Let no such man be trusted."

He is a fortunate man who occasionally escapes from his vocation. The more gripping the vocation, the more frequently should he escape from it and come to know the recreative power of the many avenues that God has put at the common call of all His servants.

CHAPTER FIFTEEN

THE SOCIETIES OF THE CHURCH

THE relief map of a congregation of a generation ago reveals quite a different picture from
that of the same congregation in the present generation. In the former there were few elevations; in fact, generally only two, the Sunday
morning service, standing out supreme, and the
instruction of young people in the afternoon, a
close second. Perhaps there was a third, the mid-
week prayer meeting. Throughout the week
there would be no other service except on very
high festival occasions. This had been the fashion
of the Protestant Church ever since her beginnings. But lo! how things have changed in the
past three decades! In addition to those two
weekly peaks there now have come to be so many
elevations that their bases often collide. This
situation has arisen from the innumerable societies that have come to aid, sometimes to clog,
the program of the Christian Church. This finally
had its highest expression in a church like St.
George's Episcopal Church, New York, with its
large and complicated institutional program.
There were night schools for the development of
men and women in any handicraft they might

choose. Our own inimitable Dr. George U.
Wenner was once asked by a parishioner for a
letter of transfer to such a congregation. He
wrote in this wise: "Mr. Jones desires a letter
to ———— Church. He desires to become a
plumber!" Smaller parishes try to do the same
work, and frequently with tragic result. The
movement in recent years throughout Christian
congregations has been toward increasing organizations; wheels within wheels have multi-
plied. This coincides with the development in
our modern life, in which people must constantly
be doing things. In the Church it is the Martha
spirit instead of the Mary spirit. Members are
bound by common action, not by common faith.
It is so much in the spirit of our modern Church
life that one must guard against this tendency,
where organizations develop in the Church as
weeds do in a garden.

When one thinks of the number of organizations that continue one can let one's imagination
survey those which have begun and were soon
done for. There are many societies in churches
that start with great enthusiasm and languish as
soon as the name and the constitution have been
adopted. It requires a wise pastor to put the
brake on this overorganization of the church, but
in doing so he will spare himself many heart-
aches and reserve for himself the energy that is
constantly being taken from his real duties. One
cannot emphasize enough the need for the min-

ister to turn almost cruelly away from many of these attempts to create new societies. They are the temptations that draw him away from his study in the morning and from his parish work in the afternoon.

But there is still added hardship when in these organizations there develop strife and bitterness. From out of the choir or the woman's society there may start a rift that will rend asunder the entire congregation. These are the things that cause restless nights and which make concentration impossible for study in the morning.

There are congregations so organized that on looking over the calendar one scarcely sees the services of worship. One looks over that same calendar, and there are so many heads of organizations that one can scarcely find the name of the pastor. It is much better to organize new groups slowly and only after a survey of those who will compose the organization and the work they plan to do. Under no consideration should an organization be created until there is some efficient, loyal person who will be the leader of that organization. If the conduct of the group must depend upon the pastor he should not permit its organization. The success of the pastor depends in part upon the responsible men and women he has to guide these new groups.

Time and again the success of a congregation is judged by the number of the organizations that

are scheduled on its programs.   The value of the
pastor is judged by them.   On the other hand, I
feel that several strong organizations in a parish
will do more for the building up of that parish
than three times the number of struggling organizations.   In the normal congregation no
society should organize to do anything that is
done so much better by secular organizations;
otherwise, by comparison the Church will reveal
herself as the weaker and men will lose confidence in her.   The Church through her organizations should do only those things which belong
to her sphere, and which no other organization
can do as well.   Here, of course, comes the purpose of practically every society in the church
to assist the church in its financial support.
When the congregation rids itself of this method
of financing it will make a tremendous stride forward.   It is unjust that women's societies in the
church should bear the major part of the church
budget, and it also creates another group of
Christians that does not in the least understand
its Christian responsibility.   There are many
organizations composed of most loyal and self-
sacrificing women who would be grieved to discover that they are doing the church more harm
than good by their generous and self-effacing
gifts.   If the purpose of societies is purely the
raising of money they had better dissolve and
leave the support of the congregation to the individual members.   Societies may still profitably

exist in congregations, but they should have one of three purposes: they should be either educational—every organization should have its educational program—or social, or means toward useful activity. It is right that the Church should have social functions. Holy Writ frequently mentions the Church as the family, and it is fitting that at times Church societies should develop this family feeling by conducting programs that bring the members to a more friendly relationship with one another. If the church dinner accomplishes this, it should be held. If attractive programs can be arranged for young people, this should be done. All things should be done decently and in order. The other purpose of the church society is its useful activity, and each organization should have some outlet for its energies. It may be a canvass of the neighborhood to enlist more people for the church's program; it may be the helping of the needy within its parish or in some more distant section. It may be the carrying out of the Church's missionary program. It can be the linking up of some civic or national enterprise that will result in good to man. Such are some of the directions our organizations may follow.

CHAPTER SIXTEEN

"THERE WERE GIANTS . . ."

ONE never ceases wondering what the stature of one's youthful heroes would be if they were alive today. And it is very difficult to measure heroes for anyone else; everybody's yardstick is different. For this reason I would list this group of giants as men who have influenced me. Needless to say, the first was my father, who during his one pastorate of forty-six years had a real pastoral heart for everyone who sought his help. I learned of the problems he faced, many of which were very real; but the influence of his home was ever positively to turn his three sons to the ministry.

Of the many episodes in my father's vigorous training for life the one I cherish most, and never fail to recall when I pass the little town of Lenhartsville, is that of his alighting here from the train, on returning home from his first year at school, and walking with the trunk on his back the distance of five miles to the farm where his father and mother were living. A giant in physique as well as in character!

In our section of the country there were other "circuit-riders" like my father—working to a large degree under a poor Church administration—who were equally faithful to their difficult duties. The Lutheran Church and the Reformed Church were the predominant affiliations. In the Reformed Church there ran parallel to my father's ministry that of the Rev. Thomas C. Leinbach, whose sermons were eagerly listened to, and who gave two splendid sons to the ministry. Fourteen miles from my home was the city of Reading, which was the metropolis of the first period of my life. In the pastor of historic Trinity Church was a giant who had both my father's and my own admiration, the Rev. Dr. Jacob Fry. He had great gifts as a preacher and as an administrator. He was looked up to by the men of affairs who comprised his official board. For thirty years he preached from that pulpit, and I was later again to meet him as professor of homiletics at the Theological Seminary in Philadelphia.

My entry into a larger life came when I went to Muhlenberg College at Allentown. It is a testimony to the personalities with whom I came in contact that this freedom for a young man at the age of fourteen was not abused. With President Theodore L. Seip, who in all his comings and goings was a Christian gentleman, as well as with the professors, one formed friendships from which one did not readily escape. Although as students we did not value the fine culture and consecration of Dr. Wackernagel, I have since come to realize that he was my first introduction to the treasure of thought which Germany gave to the world. The Rev. Dr. Stephen A. Repass, pastor of the college church, brought to the community the courteous gifts of a Southern gentleman.

My sphere was ever widening, and the opportunities brought me by my residence in Philadelphia during my theological training were eagerly seized. At the head of the faculty stood Dr. Henry Eyster Jacobs, who was master in many departments of theology. He continued until the day of his death to be a constant source of wonder to his students. In Dr. Adolph Spaeth I had the further enlargement of German culture which had begun in my college training. What a richness was spread out before the theological students in the City of Brotherly Love! There was the Church of the Holy Communion, of which the pastor was the Rev. Dr. Joseph A. Seiss, a great preacher and a prolific writer. At St. Mark's Church there was the Rev. Dr. Samuel Laird, who as president of the Ministerium of Pennsylvania ordained me to the ministry in 1899. I did not limit myself to Lutheran churches but visited churches of every denomination. At the Second Presbyterian Church in Germantown there was then the Rev. Dr. Charles Wood, eloquent preacher and popular lecturer. Twenty-five years after I went through the Holy Land with him. Dr. Francis Landey Patton was then president of Princeton University. His frequent sermons in Philadelphia would invariably draw our students.

During those closing years of the nineteenth century the fight against Tammany Hall became intense in New York. The fight was led largely by the Rev. Dr. Charles H. Parkhurst, pastor of the Madison Square Presbyterian Church. Early one October morning I took a train to New York to hear Dr. Parkhurst preach a sermon on the natural depravity of mankind that I have never forgotten. Although he read his sermon, it was delivered with such eloquence that it could not but affect every one of his hearers. At that time I was not conscious of the fact that New York was to be my permanent home. When I was asked to come to Brooklyn to conduct mission work the attraction of the great Brooklyn preachers played no small part with me. Before I actually arrived, however, Beecher was dead, Storrs had retired, and Cuyler preached but rarely. I came to know this last of the triumvirate, and recalled with him many of the things my father had told me of him. Although these three giants had gone, never to be replaced in the City of Churches, the fervor they had created in the Church life of the city did not wane, at least during my thirteen years' pastorate.

The man in New York who came to have a tremendous influence upon me through his unique pastorate was the Rev. George U. Wenner, who held the longest pastorate of any man in the City of Skyscrapers, organizing his work on the East Side in 1868 and not relinquishing the pastorate until his death in 1934. He was especially hospitable to young men and encouraged those who saw in New York the greatest challenge of the age to the Christian Church. He was active in the work of the Church at large and faithful in his own parish in the gashouse district of New York. The sweetest story told of him is that of a man who had been run down by a streetcar, and in his extreme moments asked to see the pastor who published the *Sonntags Gast,* the family religious paper which Dr. Wenner published every week, and which the man had in his pocket at the time of the accident.

Then there was the scholarly and dignified Rev. G. F. Krotel, called to organize Holy Trinity Church on West Twenty-First Street, and later to be pastor of the Church of the Advent. It was a pleasure to listen to these men and to hear tales of the men who had preceded them. Dr. Wenner would proudly say he knew every Lutheran minister in New York, save six or seven, for one hundred years. In knowing some of these giants I felt myself a coworker in the work of the past century.

On the upper East Side was the Rev. J. B. Remensnyder, pastor of St. James's Church, who was prolific in his writings in defense of the Church. Belonging to that same circle was the Rev. Dr. G. C. Berkemeier, director of the Wartburg Orphans Home, a preacher and poet in both German and English.

But I was soon drawn in with the organizers of the new New York and New England Synod, and in this way I became still further associated with strong, consecrated men. At the western end of the State there was the Rev. Dr. F. A. Kahler, whose parish in Buffalo was not simply that of a congregation but the entire city. His fifty years' ministry there was one of the outstanding pastorates of the Church. In Rochester the ministry of the Rev. Dr. Franklin F. Fry was remarkable; it can be said to be as nearly perfect as that of any man in the Church, both in preaching and in administration. In Utica there was the Rev. Frank Klingensmith, whose precarious health compelled him to cut short an otherwise brilliant ministry. In New York there was the amiable and studious Pastor C. Armand Miller, and in Brooklyn Pastor Samuel Weiskotten, who with Pastors Knabenschuh and Steimle took advantage of former Mayor Schieren's aid to accomplish one of the most striking mission advances in the history of the Church. Later this group was joined by the Rev. William M. Horn, who through his outstanding native gifts, by his far-seeing vision, and by his knowledge of men has left his influence along many avenues in the Church.

For six years the room in the Lutheran Church House which I occupied as president of the

Synod adjoined that of Dr. M. G. G. Scherer, first secretary of the United Lutheran Church in America. He was a man of profound scholarship, yet tolerant and conciliatory toward those who differed from him. His gentle, warmhearted manner invited confidence. When he died in 1932 his loss was felt throughout the Church.

During the many years of my life in New York I was a member of the Philothean Society, a limited circle of pastors of various churches who met on Saturday evening for dinner and the discussion of some paper. The warm friendships of this circle was one of the greatest influences of my life. The circle included the Rev. Cornelius Woelfkin, of the Fifth Avenue Baptist Church, the Rev. George P. Eckman, editor of the Methodist *Christian Advocate,* the Rev. Henry M. Sanders, minister-at-large for the Baptist Church, the Rev. Henry Stimson, pastor of the Manhattan Congregational Church, and Canon Douglas of the Episcopal Church. At times I can recognize these men in parts of my thinking.

I have always regretted not having heard Phillips Brooks preach, but I have pictured him standing in Trinity pulpit at the head of Wall Street, preaching those Lenten sermons to congregations of men, congregations that flowed over into that historic churchyard. The Presbyterian Church has had the outstanding preachers in New York during my time. At the Brick Church there was the Rev. Dr. Henry Van

Dyke, whom I later came to know at Bar Harbor; I also became acquainted with his successor the Rev. Maltbie D. Babcock. But the Fifth Avenue Presbyterian Church was the haven for preachers. During the winter I had no opportunity to visit other churches, but in the summer visiting English preachers would draw tremendous congregations at this center of great preaching. I have known the three great English preachers there in the past twenty-five years —the silver-tongued Jowett, whom I first met crossing to England for the coronation of King George V; John Kelman, poet-preacher of Edinburgh; and Henry Howard of Australia. Each of these men had a deep spiritual culture, and would open to us the hidden things of God in a way that at times seemed incredible.

When I went to France in 1917 I had new contacts with preachers. Some of them suffered cruelly, robbed of their setting of church and pulpit. It surely was a testing time for the Church; often she failed of being the victor. There were, however, men of God who triumphed by their consecrated personalities over the confusion and upheaval of war. Bishop Charles H. Brent, of the Episcopal Church, who was the head of the chaplains' corps, afterwards worked side by side with me in Buffalo as Bishop of Western New York. With the Presiding Bishop of the Episcopal Church, James De Wolf Perry, there began a friendship which has been

growing ever since. Father Duffy, of the famous
Sixty-ninth Regiment of New York, was considered the best chaplain in the service. With a
remarkable boyish quality he entered into all the
legitimate enjoyments of the soldier, but always
remained the spiritual adviser of his boys, who
would go to him as to a father. At his death I
was privileged to broadcast over WOR a tribute
to him from the Protestant churches.

Among world leaders in the Christian Church
I have counted many as friends. I have already
spoken of the outstanding figure of the evangelical world during the past generation, Archbishop Soderblom. At the time when I became
acquainted with him I first met Bishop Ihmels
of Saxony, who was a giant in his thinking and
deeply devoted to the truth. Bishop Lunde, the
Primate of Norway, and Bishop Ostenfeld, Primate of Denmark, have visited America in the
past decade and helped to cement our relations
with the great peoples they represented.

At the recent Third World Convention of the
Lutheran Church in Paris I felt the affairs of the
Church were in the hands of able men of the
younger generation from whom in years to come
would develop many giants in the work of God's
Kingdom. As to those who are alive and active
in the Vineyard, it must be left to a future his-
torian to decide who shall be counted among the
noble band. Of this one thing I am certain, God
does not leave Himself without witness in any age.

CHAPTER SEVENTEEN

LOOKING BACK

THE plowman will look back over the field to see whether he has plowed a straight furrow. So every man at times in his life, and especially at the completion of certain periods, will look back to discern crooked places that might have been straightened and hills that should have been made plain. There seemed to be a special drive that sought to get me into active life at an early age. With this my father was thoroughly in sympathy, and I rather enjoyed the exhilaration. I entered college at the age of fourteen, and had little difficulty in making good marks. It was a youthful mind that lapped up everything within reach. One thing my college training failed to do for me—it failed to produce reflective thinking. Had I taken that same training four years later I should have approached it from an entirely different angle. At present there are various vocations to which a boy can apply himself while he is waiting a fit age to enter college. I believe that going out into the world and taking some job would have been better for me than to have taken a training for which I was not yet ready. However, I entered the ministry at the age of twenty-one, and had an enthusiasm for my work which might not have been mine had I been older in years. Then I would have taken graduate work either after my college course or after my seminary experience for a year or two. Years in the ministry normally do not differ very much from one another, they follow in regular succession. But how much each one of those years would have been enriched had I taken graduate work at some advanced institution in this country, or, possibly, in England or on the continent of Europe. I am very much of the conviction that there are periods in life for doing each specific thing. Special study will mean much at any time in a minister's life, but how much more his life would mean if he entered his vocation with a rich preparation, retaining the benefit of it throughout his ministry! I have the same conviction in regard to travel; it should begin early so that it will color and leaven all the things a man does afterwards. If I had my early days to live again I would change my mental habits. In the enthusiasm of missionary work it was easy to spend my whole day and part of the night out on the field, calling upon people and in turn securing their interest in the Church. I now believe I would have done those people a greater service had I imprisoned myself for the entire morning in my study, therein developing my mental and spiritual life so as to be of more lasting value to my people. That cloistered morning must be guarded against every intruder by the minister who desires genuinely to help his people.

When I finished my course in college I turned over in my mind the problem of my vocation. Preponderant influences were at work to send me into the ministry but, as I have already noted, I gave some attention to law so that there might be some other claim, the value of which I could then test. As I look back I believe that the one barrier preventing me from going immediately into the ministry was the quality of some of the men who had preceded me or were then candidates. However, the ministry won out; and I have never regretted this decision.

'Whether I should take a country parish or become enmeshed in city work required a decision almost as great as the previous one. My father would have been very happy had I accepted a parish like his; we should then have been co-workers and have had the intimate touch a father naturally desires with his son. However, there was no call to such a parish, and the time of my ordination drew on rapidly without any indication as to my field of work. I have since come to trust the providential hand of God in man's affairs, and each step in my life has been taken with strong forces impelling me on rather than of my own choice. A week before my graduation from the theological school a committee from Brooklyn came to see me and immediately planned to have me do mission work in that city, then so ripe for mission work. The question was solved for me, although it made my father and myself gasp that things had so soon taken a turn we had not expected. I have sometimes pictured myself in a small town where I might more readily have found myself, and where I would have had time for study. A parish such as this is ideal for a young man if he has the determination to guard himself against the easier demands of a parish which needs but to be kept alive.

I sailed to France as a chaplain with the Army with that same feeling of forces behind me, which I could not counteract. There seemed to be no choice. With high exaltation of feeling my congregation of the Church of the Redeemer, Buffalo, granted me permission to serve with the Army as long as was necessary. This apparently would be for but a brief period, but I was absent from my parish for almost two years. In the light of the finer thinking that has taken hold of men since the World War I wonder whether I might not at this time have a different attitude. In even the most conscientious chaplain during the war there was too much of partisan incitement, too little of ministry in the name of the Nazarene Whose conquering weapon is love.

With the same yielding to forces over which I had no control I was taken out of a parish that was humanly speaking well-nigh perfect to take over executive work as president of the Synod of New York and New England. It came like a thunderclap in a clear sky when the Synod decided that it would have a full-time president and that I should be the president. My first Sunday's visitation was to a congregation where the pastor desired to use his tenth anniversary to give new inspiration to his lagging work. He was an altogether commendable man of fine spirit, but lacking in certain qualities in his temperament, which made it impossible for him to work with his congregation. At the same time a committee from the congregation besought me to find some other parish for him. Here was a problem that confronted me when I was fresh from a unified, harmonious, and aggressive work. For four years I tried to place that man in some other parish. Since that time I have been compelled to face similar problems again and again. Sometimes I have wondered whether I had chosen in accordance with my best interests, but there were forces which could not be gainsaid. I still believe that the work of the pastor is the most important and also the most satisfying in the Church. What a joy it is to see the unfolding of families starting a new life that gives promise of a better world; to feel the confidence and affection of a congregation, rejoicing with those that rejoice, weeping with those that weep, running the gamut of human experiences! In a parish this contact is much closer and more readily directed than in any executive position. Besides this, there is the companionship of one's books in the study, a companionship quite impossible when one travels over great distances by motor-car or train. But all these changes in my life were not of my making, they were in the control of a stronger Hand than mine. It never would have occurred to me voluntarily to relinquish my executive work as president of the Synod, but now that I have been released from this position I find in that release the working of those same forces that determined my life in other crises. With the leisure that has come to me for reading, travel, study, and meditation I am coming to have a clearer grasp of the increasing and per-plexing problems of the Church.

CHAPTER EIGHTEEN

"THIS ONE THING I DO"

THE captain of a transatlantic liner expects new experiences with every voyage. This makes each crossing stand out by itself. He will make new friends, and he will meet new problems. Storms may arise that will go beyond anything he has previously known; he may even be led out of his course for an entire day to rescue an imperiled ship. He may make minor calls at ports of less importance, but the purpose of his vessel is not accomplished until he docks her, and lands her passengers, at her European port or in New York. He keeps this goal in mind; everything contributes to that goal. Even before he leaves port every preparation for the sailing has that purpose in view. The ship is loaded with oil and provisions, and manned so that it shall safely bring its freight to the other side. The stalwart skipper never ceases to be a romantic figure because of his knowing the whole world; and yet at that sailing he has but one port in mind. It is a remarkable instance of concentration. It is that which St. Paul had in mind when he wrote to the Philippians, "This one thing I do." The minister of God must have in his own consciousness that same concentrated purpose if he would fulfill his vocation.

Although the commander of the vessel will always have his charts before him, he knows the path of the seas so well that normally he can follow his course without using them. The ambassador of Christ must have before him his well-worn chart. As each new day comes he must wrestle in prayer until his vocation again stands out clearly. What is the day for unless it is for the fulfilling of his vocation as a minister of God? It is well to define this vocation for himself at each day's opening, and it will be well, when the heat and the fever of the day have passed over, if he asks himself whether he has accomplished that vocation. In this way the purpose of his vocation becomes stronger with each passing year, and his vocation will finally master him. There is no other group of men who are so easily led astray in this matter as are ministers. One cannot accuse them of being less busy than other men. In fact, the normal minister's day counts more than the six, eight, ten, or even twelve hours of the regular workman's day. His time is not his own, and the finer the sense of his obligation, the more is he in danger of scattering his energies over the map of man's interests. He can be busy all day with causes none of which has any real relation to his vocation. He is the willing horse who consents to take any cause in the community that no one else cares to take upon himself. The physician, the lawyer, the teacher, each has his distinct vocation; they are not called upon to squander their energies. The minister with an indifferent sense of his vocation takes upon himself every cause, and fails to accomplish the one thing that his vocation asks.

I recently heard of a man whose vocation consisted in the firing of a cannon at noonday in the park of the city where he lived. This man could easily have taken on other objectives; as it was, his life narrowed down to that one shot at noon each day. The minister of Jesus Christ, who has the glorious objective of bringing man to know Him Who is the Way, the Truth, and the Life, that man cannot go into all types of extraneous activity.

In a letter written by George Whitefield to a friend on the day of his ordination occurs the following sublime and comprehensive, yet simple, expression: "I hope the good of souls will be my only principle of action. I call Heaven and earth to witness that when the bishop laid his hand upon me I gave myself like a martyr for Him Who hung upon the cross for me." Men will look at a minister and will say either, "He is just another clergyman," or, sensing his inner purpose, "There is a minister of God."

The chief object of the study of this minister of God is to be Christ and His mind for us. Other subjects will have value only as they bring light to this inexhaustible subject. The purpose of preaching is to reveal Christ to those who hear the message. Other subjects will have place only as they help toward this end. It is not to be simply the rules of life that are to form the Christian message but it is the presence of this sublime Helper Who transforms us that we may be able to live in this better way. Alexis Carrel, whom I first came to know twenty years ago crossing to Europe on the *France,* and whom I have since followed with great interest, says in his book, *Man the Unknown:* "Ministers have rationalized religion. They have destroyed its mystical basis. But they do not succeed in attracting modern men. In their half-empty churches they vainly preach a weak morality. They are content with the part of policemen, helping in the interest of the wealthy to preserve the framework of present society. Or, like politicians, they flatter the appetites of the crowd."

The "one thing" we who are pastors are doing is to strive by God's grace to make men know Christ, in Whom alone is the hope of the world. This we cannot accomplish unless Christ Himself lives in us. This we share in common with every one of the souls intrusted to us. "What you are comes before what you do," someone has said. This brings to us the primary purpose of the minister's life. He must be so convinced of the truth that he preaches, and of the life that he lives, that he cannot but communicate this to everyone with whom he comes in contact.